Consulting Authors

Richard G. Boehm, Professor
Director of the Grosvenor Center for Geographic Education, and Jesse H. Jones Distinguished Chair in Geographic Education
Southwest Texas State University
San Marcos, Texas

Brenda Webb, Assistant Professor
Kilby Laboratory School
University of North Alabama
Florence, Alabama

Columbus, OH • Chicago, IL • Redmond, WA

The McGraw·Hill Companies

TABLE OF CONTENTS

Map Skills

TABLE OF CONTENTS

Reading and Thinking Skills

Writing and Research Skills

TABLE OF CONTENTS

Chart and Graph Skills

Test-Taking Strategies

Map Skills

Skill 1

HOW TO Read a Map

Map Magic

Did you know that the whole United States can fit on one piece of paper? It sounds like magic, but it can happen on a map.

A **map** is a flat drawing that shows what a real place looks like from above. Maps can use lines, shapes, and colors to show information about parts of the world.

There are many kinds of maps and many reasons why people use them. A bus driver may use maps to find streets. A city planner may use maps to plan parks in a community. You may use a map to learn more about the United States.

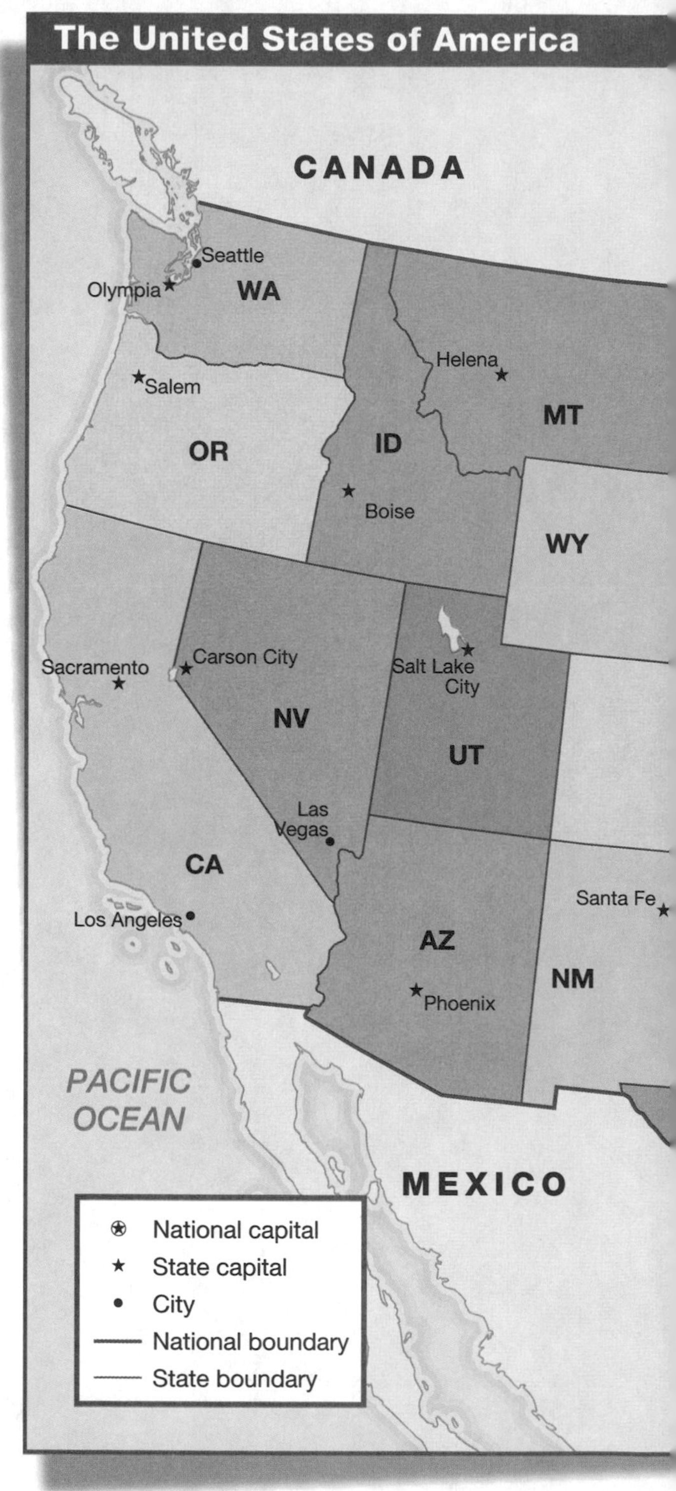

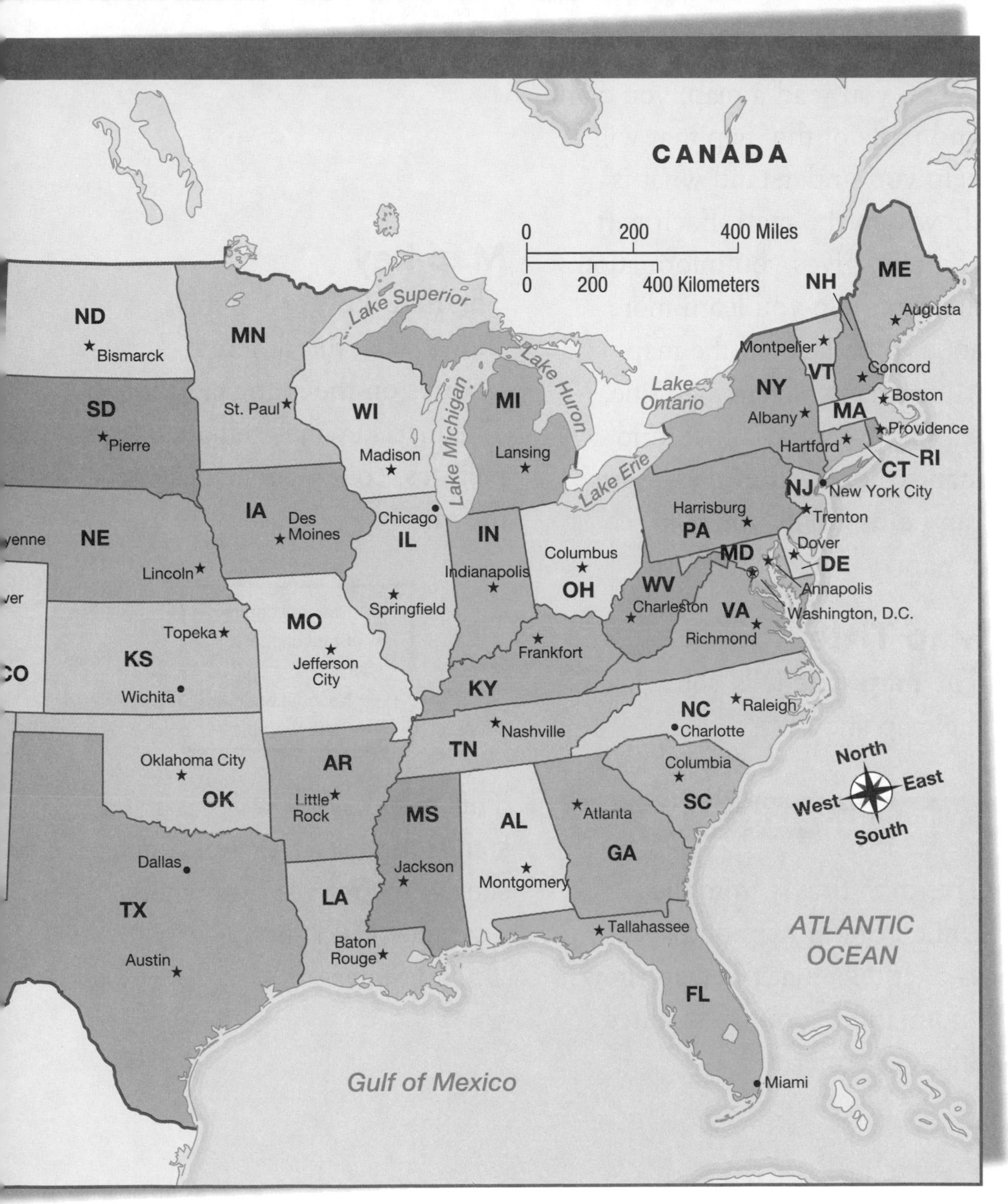

CANADA
0
200
400 Miles
0
200
400 Kilometers
Lake Superior
Lake Michigan
Lake Huron
Lake Ontario
Lake Erie
ND
Bismarck
MN
St. Paul
SD
Pierre
WI
Madison
MI
Lansing
IA
Des Moines
NE
Lincoln
yenne
ver
CO
KS
Topeka
Wichita
MO
Jefferson City
IL
Chicago
Springfield
IN
Indianapolis
OH
Columbus
KY
Frankfort
WV
Charleston
VA
Richmond
PA
Harrisburg
NY
Albany
VT
Montpelier
NH
Concord
ME
Augusta
MA
Boston
RI
Providence
CT
Hartford
NJ
Trenton
New York City
DE
Dover
MD
Annapolis
Washington, D.C.
NC
Raleigh
Charlotte
TN
Nashville
SC
Columbia
GA
Atlanta
AL
Montgomery
MS
Jackson
AR
Little Rock
LA
Baton Rouge
OK
Oklahoma City
TX
Dallas
Austin
FL
Tallahassee
Miami
North
East
West
South
ATLANTIC OCEAN
Gulf of Mexico

When you read a map, you can find parts of the map that will help you understand what is shown on the map. Each part of a map gives you information that can help you learn more about the place on the map. Many maps have a map title, map key, compass rose, and map scale. Each of these parts can be useful as you read a map.

Map Title

The **map title** tells you what the map shows.

The United States of America

This map title is from the United States map on pages 4–5. It tells that the map shows information about the United States of America.

Map Key

The **map key,** or **legend,** shows what the different features on the map stand for. The map key may tell about the pictures, colors, or shapes on the map.

⍟	National capital
★	State capital
•	City
——	National boundary
——	State boundary

This map key shows that a star stands for a state capital. Each star on the map shows where a state capital is in the United States.

Compass Rose

The **compass rose** shows directions on a map. It tells which places are north, south, east, or west of other places. On most maps, North is at the top of the page.

By using the compass rose on the United States map, you can see that South Dakota (SD) is north of Kansas (KS). You can also see that Maine (ME) is east of Washington (WA).

Map Scale

The **map scale** is a line that helps measure distance on a map. It tells how the distance between places or things on a map compares to the distance between the real places or things.

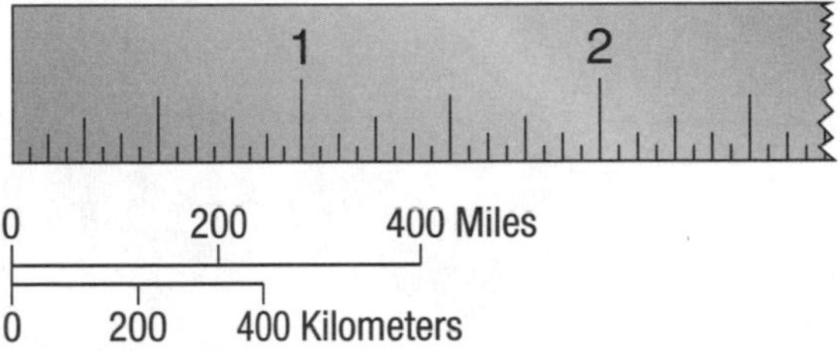

This map scale lets you find distances between places or things on the United States map. You can measure the distance between Boise, Idaho (ID), and Helena, Montana (MT), with a ruler. By putting the ruler next to the map scale, you can see that one inch on the map equals about 300 miles. The cities are one inch apart on the map so you can tell that the real cities are about 300 miles apart.

The map below shows some western states in the United States. Think about what each part of the map tells you about the western states shown on the map.

USE THIS SKILL

Read a Map

Use the map on page 8 to answer the following questions.

1. What is the title of the map?
2. How many miles equal two inches on the map?
3. How many miles apart are Sacramento, California (CA), and Carson City, Nevada (NV)?
4. What does this picture stand for on the map?
5. What is the state to the west of Nevada?
6. If you were traveling from Washington (WA) to Oregon (OR), in what direction would you be going?
7. What river runs along the state boundary between Arizona (AZ) and California (CA)?

TEST TIP **On a test, you may see a compass rose with the points labeled N, S, E, and W. These letters stand for directions. N stands for North, S for South, E for East, and W stands for West.**

Skill 2

HOW TO

Read Map Symbols

Breaking the Code

Did you know that maps often use codes to give information about a place? By learning about the symbols on a map, you can break the code.

The small drawings that are used on a map are called **symbols.** There are many different kinds of symbols. Pictures, colors, and shapes can be symbols. Symbols stand for real things. You can think of symbols like a code. The map key unlocks the code by telling what each symbol stands for on the map.

The map on this page uses colors to stand for real things.

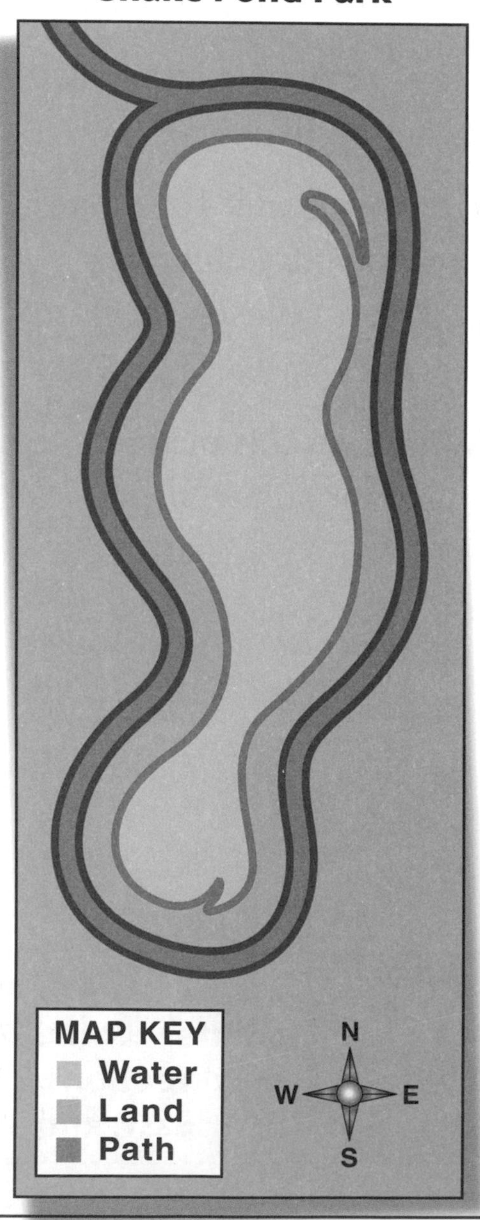

This town map uses shapes to stand for real things.

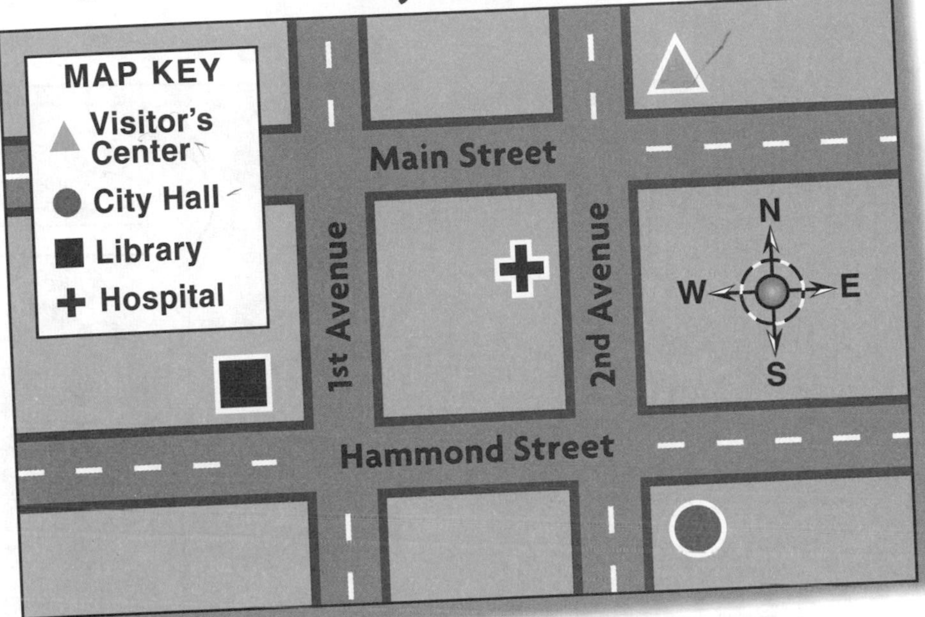

This farm map uses pictures to stand for real things.

Jones' Farm

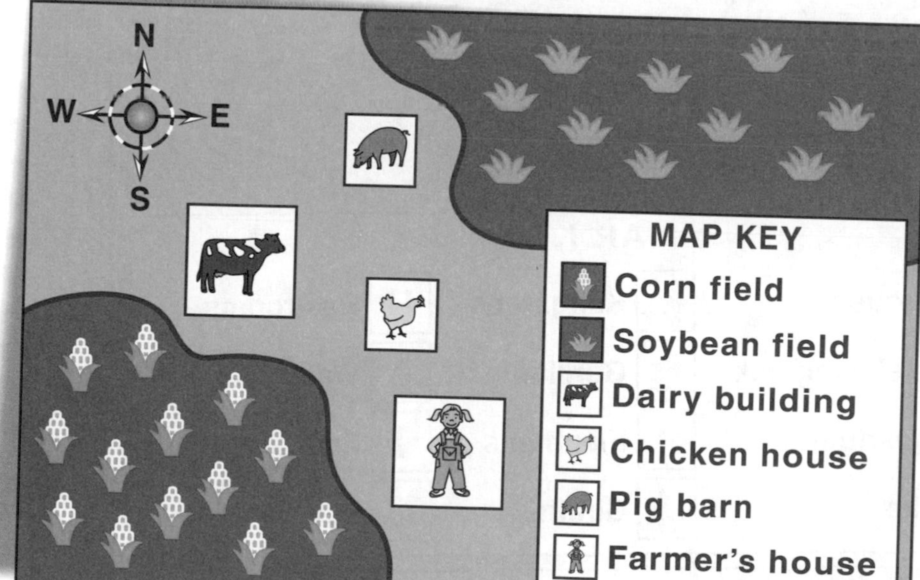

The map below shows a zoo. Think about how the symbols in the map key help you to read the zoo map.

The Zoo

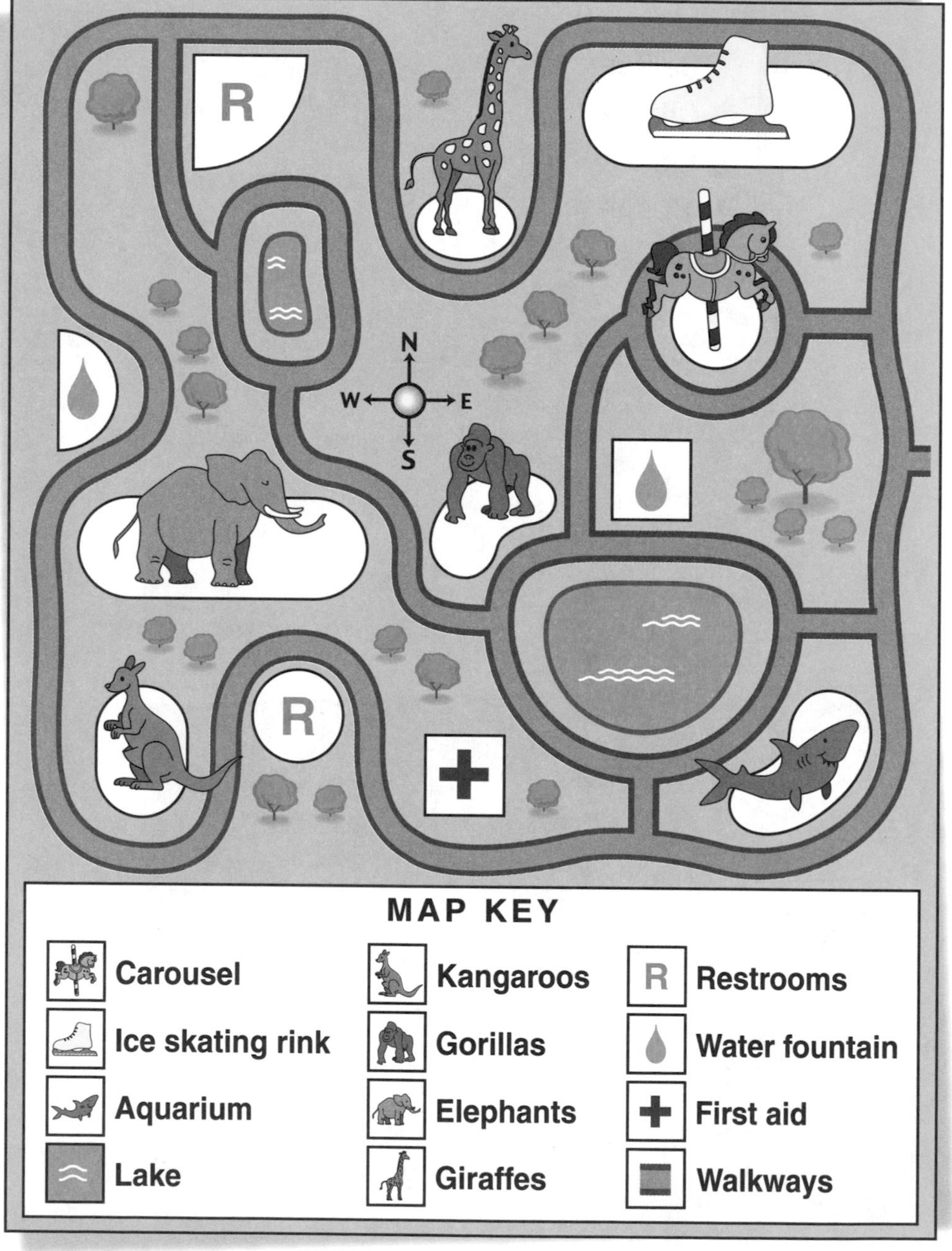

USE THIS SKILL

Read Map Symbols

Use the zoo map on page 12 to answer the questions.

1. Are the giraffes north or south of the first aid?
2. Is the aquarium east or west of the kangaroos?
3. What does [symbol] stand for on the map?
4. Suppose you were at the ice skating rink. Which direction would you walk to go to the carousel?
5. Imagine that your class wants to walk through the zoo and see all the animals shown on the map key. Using the map symbols, plan a trip for the class. Tell where the trip will start, in which directions the class should turn along the way, and where you should end the trip. Then tell the order in which you saw the zoo animals.

TEST TIP **When using a map to answer questions on a test, make sure you know what each symbol represents.**

Skill 3

HOW TO

Read a Community Map

Seaside Communities

How does a delivery person deliver packages to houses without street numbers? In the California community of Carmel-by-the-Sea, a delivery person may look for a house's name, like *Tinkerbell* or *Teapot*.

Whether a person lives in a home named *Teapot* or one with a street number, he or she lives in a community. A **community** is a place where people live, work, and play. Carmel-by-the-Sea is a small community in California by the Pacific Ocean. It is often just called Carmel.

A **community map** shows the features, or details, of a community. The community map on page 15 shows some of the places and things found in the seaside community of Carmel-by-the-Sea. You can tell that Carmel-by-the-Sea is east of Carmel Bay by looking at the map. The map also helps you find the location of places like the library and police station in the community.

TIP On a community map, the title of the map often tells the name of the community. The symbols on the map stand for real places that can be found in the community.

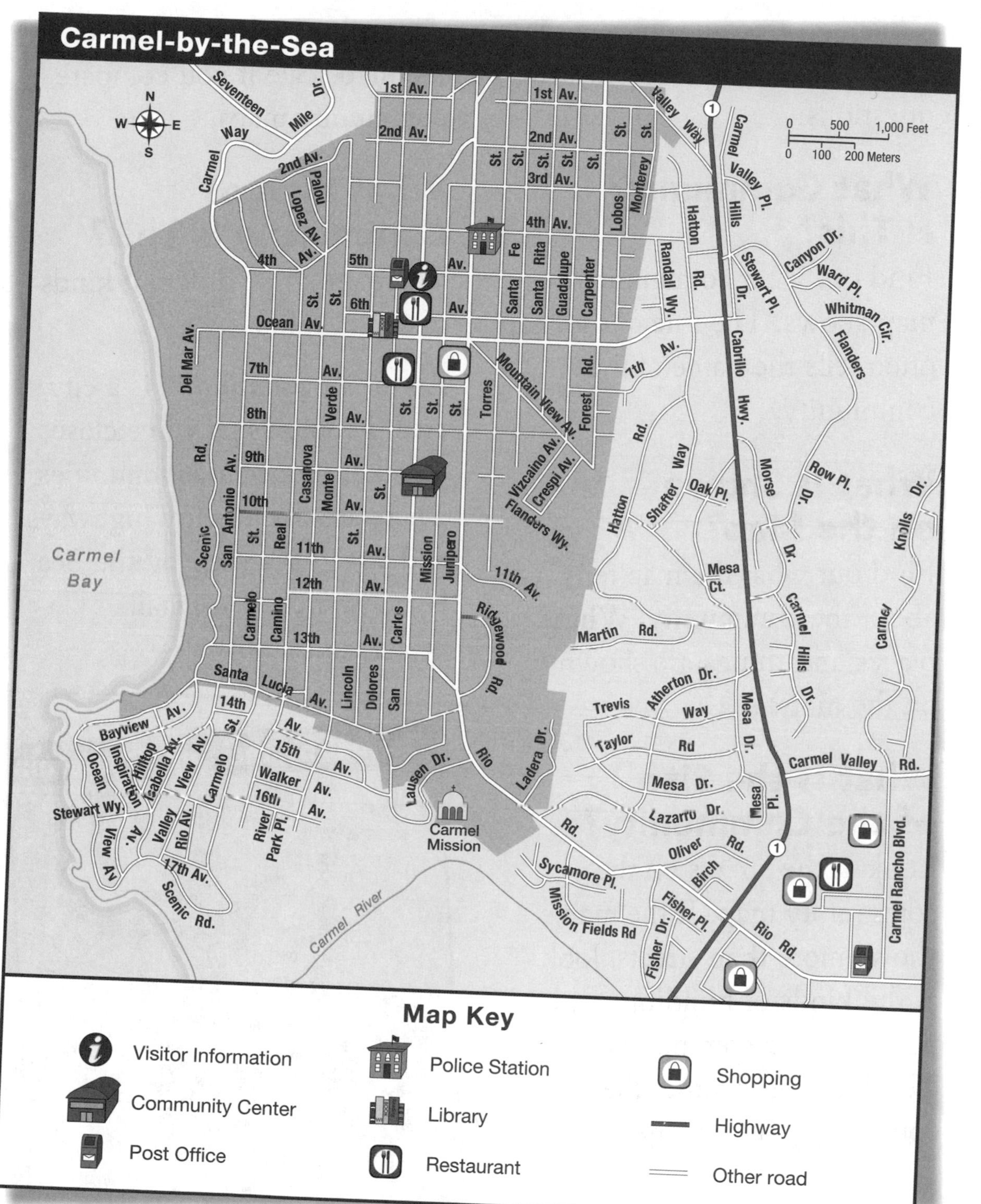

Carmel-by-the-Sea
N
S
E
W
0 500 1,000 Feet
0 100 200 Meters
Carmel Bay
Carmel River
Carmel Mission
Seventeen Mile Dr.
Carmel Way
1st Av.
2nd Av.
3rd Av.
4th Av.
5th Av.
6th Av.
Ocean Av.
7th Av.
8th Av.
9th Av.
10th Av.
11th Av.
12th Av.
13th Av.
14th
15th Av.
16th Av.
17th Av.
Valley Way
Carmel Valley Pl.
Hills Dr.
Stewart Pl.
Canyon Dr.
Ward Pl.
Whitman Cir.
Flanders
Cabrillo Hwy.
Hatton Rd.
Randall Wy.
Lobos St.
Monterey St.
Carpenter St.
Guadalupe St.
Santa Rita St.
Santa Fe St.
Del Mar Av.
Palou
Lopez Av.
Mountain View Av.
Torres St.
Forest Rd.
Vizcaino Av.
Crespi Av.
Flanders Wy.
Shafter Way
Oak Pl.
Morse Dr.
Row Pl.
Knolls Dr.
Mesa Ct.
Carmel Hills Dr.
Carmel
Scenic Rd.
San Antonio Av.
Casanova St.
Monte Verde St.
Mission St.
Junipero St.
Real
Carmelo St.
Camino
Lincoln
Dolores
San Carlos St.
Rio Rd.
Ridgewood Rd.
Martin Rd.
Atherton Dr.
Trevis Way
Taylor Rd
Mesa Dr.
Lazarro Dr.
Mesa Pl.
Carmel Valley Rd.
Carmel Rancho Blvd.
Ladera Dr.
Lausen Dr.
Santa Lucia Av.
Bayview Av.
Ocean
Inspiration
Hilltop
Isabella Av.
View Av.
Carmelo
Walker Av.
River Park Pl.
Stewart Wy.
Valley
Rio Av.
View Av
Oliver Rd.
Birch
Sycamore Pl.
Mission Fields Rd
Fisher Pl.
Fisher Dr.
Map Key
Visitor Information
Community Center
Post Office
Police Station
Library
Restaurant
Shopping
Highway
Other road

When you read a community map, ask yourself the following questions.

What Community Is This?

Find out what community the map shows. The title of the map often tells the name of the community.

What Is Shown on the Map?

Find out what the map tells about the community. What places and things are shown on the map?

What Is the Size of the Community?

Look at the streets on the community map. If the map shows more than streets, look at the kinds of buildings and homes in the community. Think about whether the community seems large or small. Be sure to look at the map scale if you compare community maps.

What Kind of Community Is This?

There are three different kinds of communities.

An urban community is a city area. People usually live close together in urban communities. There are often many highways and streets. Carmel-by-the-Sea is an example of a small urban community.

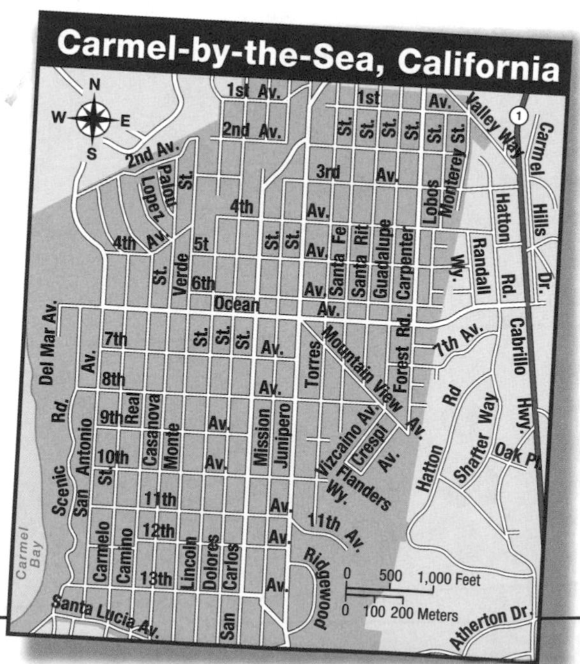

A suburban community is an area just outside of a large city. You can find suburban communities around most large cities. People who live in suburban communities often live close together, but not as closely as people living in urban communities. Burbank is an example of a suburban community just outside of the large city of Los Angeles.

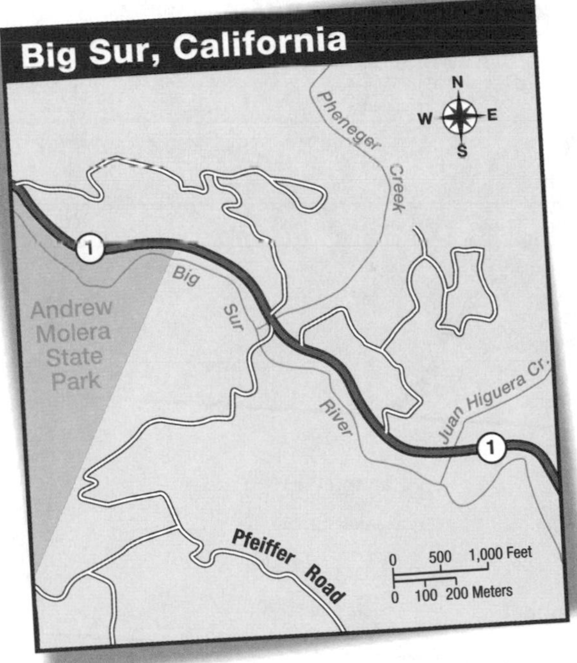

A rural community is an area with farms or open land. People live farther apart in rural communities. The highways and roads are also farther apart in rural communities. Big Sur is an example of a rural community.

The map below shows places and things in Big Sur. Think about what you can learn about the community of Big Sur from this map.

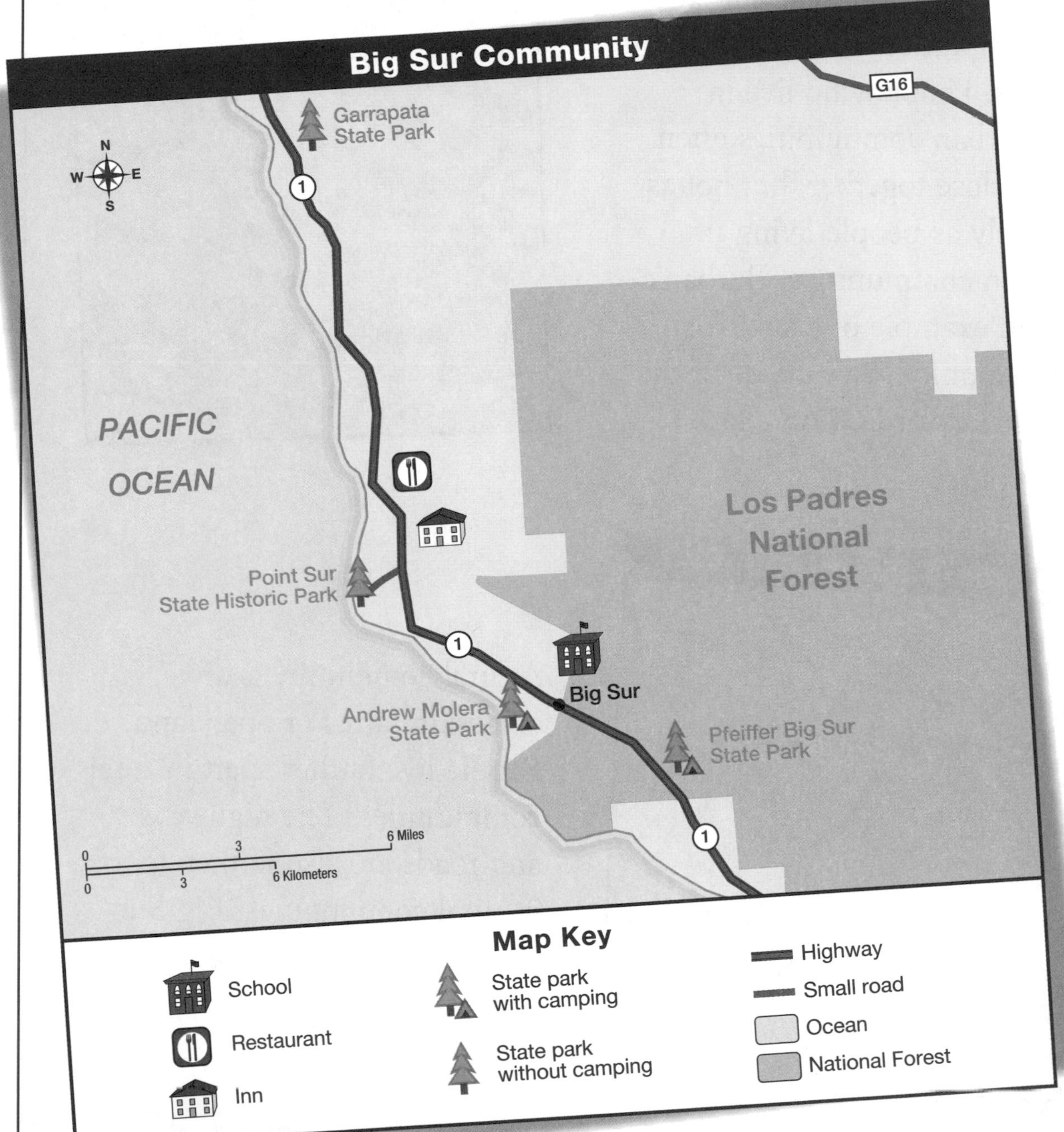

USE THIS SKILL

Read a Community Map

Use the map of Big Sur on page 18 to answer these questions.

1. What community is shown on the map?
2. How many state parks with camping are shown on the map?
3. If you were at Point Sur State Historic Park, in which direction would you go to get to Garrapata State Park?
4. Is the inn east or west of Los Padres National Forest?
5. Use the scale to tell how far Andrew Molera State Park is from the school.
6. What highway runs through part of Los Padres National Forest?
7. Suppose you were eating in the restaurant and wanted to visit the nearest state park. Which park would you visit?

TEST TIP

Some tests may ask you to use a community map to locate different places or things. Use the map's compass rose because North is not always at the top of the map.

Skill 4

HOW TO Read a State Map

Crazy about Kansas!

Where can you find the world's largest ball of twine, the world's largest coal shovel, and the place where Amelia Earhart was born? It may sound crazy, but they can all be found in Kansas.

To find out more about Kansas, you can look at a state map. A **state map** is a map that shows information about a state. The state map on the next page shows Kansas, one of the 50 United States.

Here are some things to look for when you read a state map.

Look for what the map tells about the state. The map on page 21 shows state boundaries. A **boundary** is a line where one thing ends and something else begins. State boundaries show where one state ends and another begins. The boundaries on this map show the shape of Kansas.

Look for other features. This map shows some cities of different sizes and the state capital of Kansas. It shows interstate and state highways. The map also shows where some rivers can be found in Kansas.

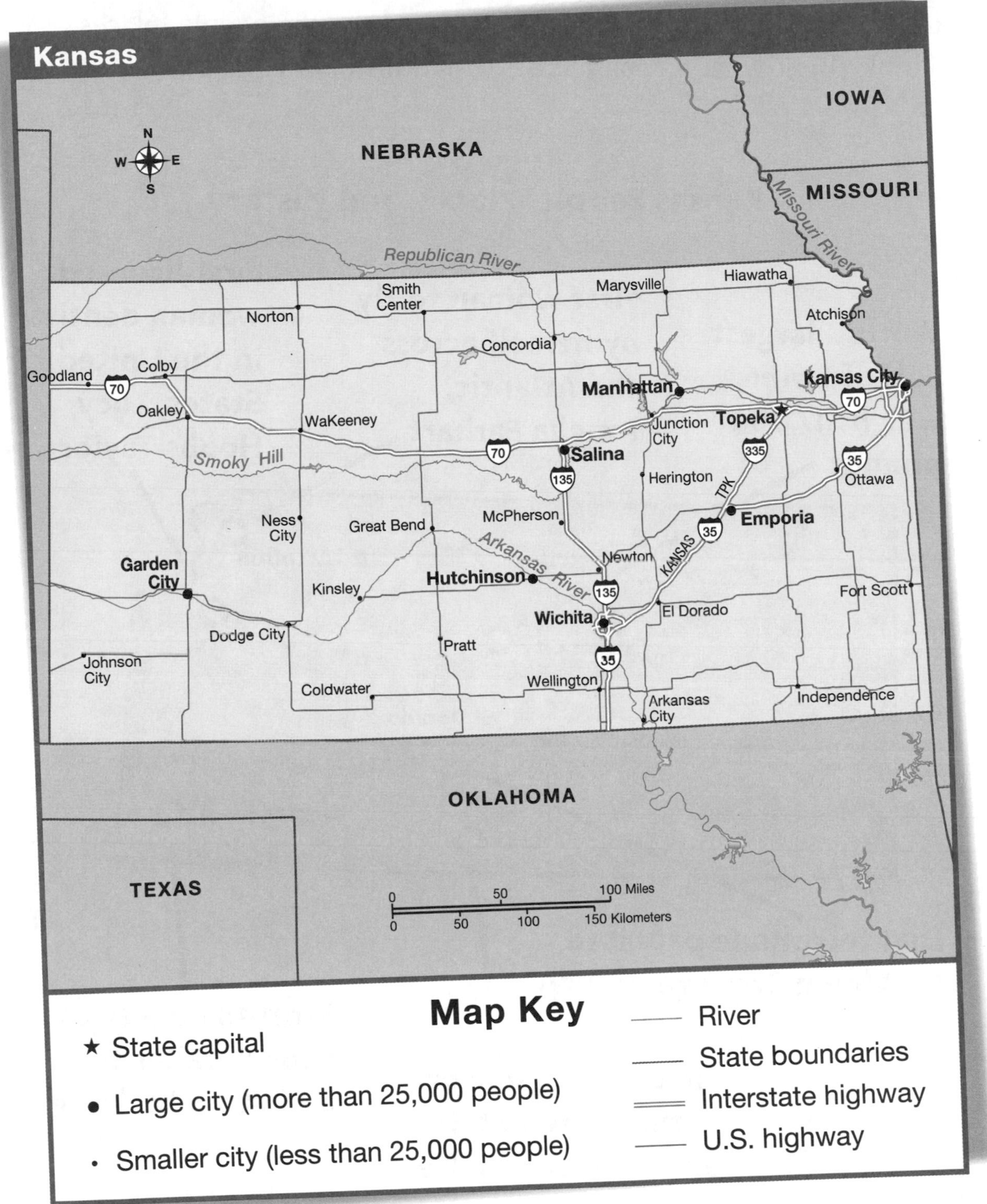

Map Key

★ State capital

● Large city (more than 25,000 people)

• Smaller city (less than 25,000 people)

River

State boundaries

Interstate highway

U.S. highway

Look at the state map below. Think about what the map tells you about the people, places, and history of Kansas.

Kansas People, Places, and History

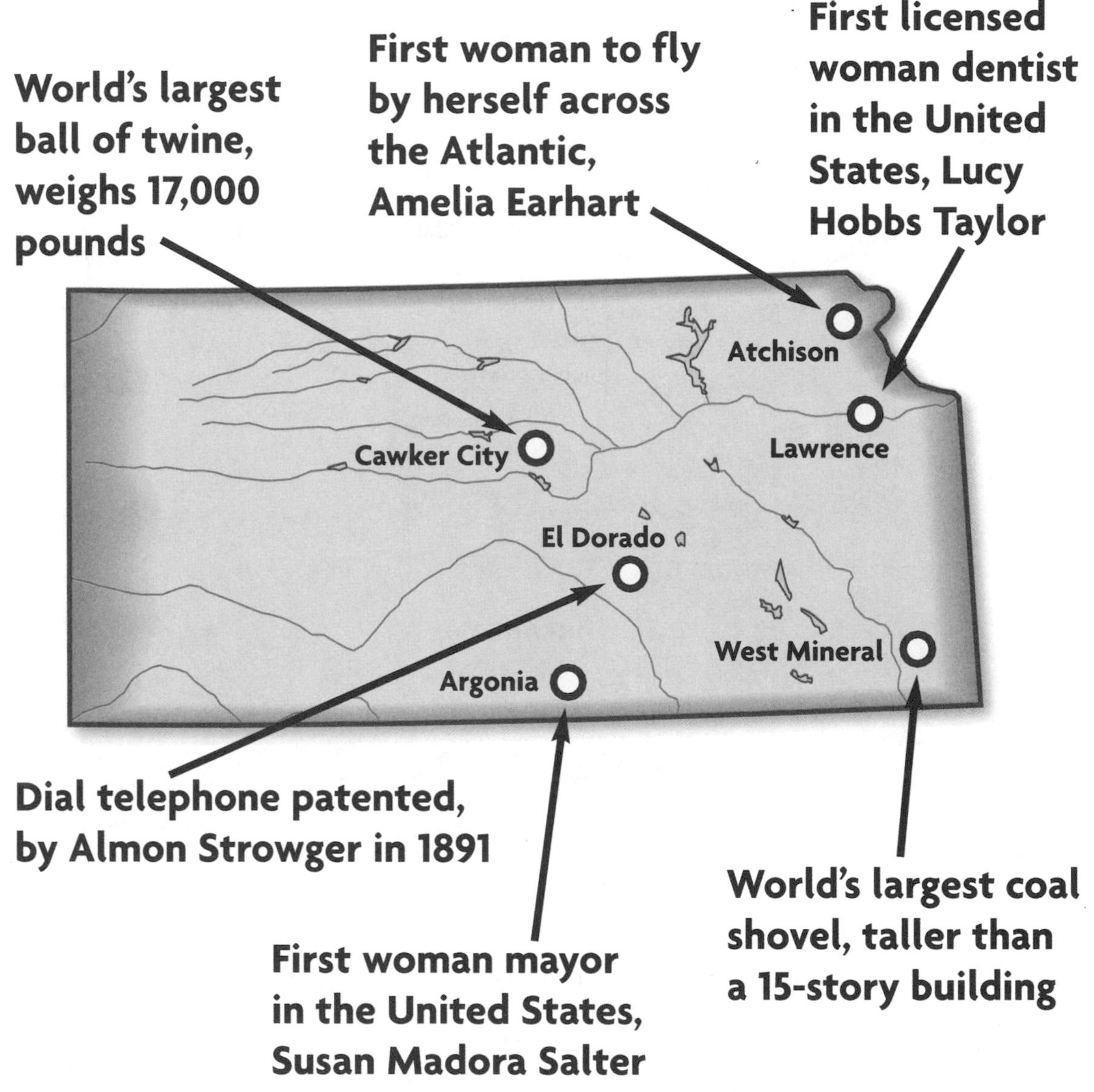

USE THIS SKILL

Read a State Map

Use the state map of Kansas on page 21 to answer the following questions.

1. Suppose you were in the city of Norton and you walked north across Kansas's state boundary. Which state would you enter?
2. What interstate highway would you take to go from Salina to Oakley?
3. What river runs beside Dodge City?
4. Based on the map key, which city is larger, Wichita or Concordia?

Use the state map of Kansas on page 22 to answer the following questions.

5. In what city was the dial telephone patented?
6. Name two people identified on this state map.
7. If you were in Lawrence, Kansas, and wanted to see the world's largest coal shovel, in which direction would you travel?

TEST TIP **When a test asks you to use a state map to answer questions, make sure to find the state's boundaries and other important places.**

Skill 5

HOW TO

Read a Country Map

Finding Your Way in the U.S.A.

Did you know that the United States is the world's fourth largest country in land area? With a country so large, directions can help you locate places in the United States.

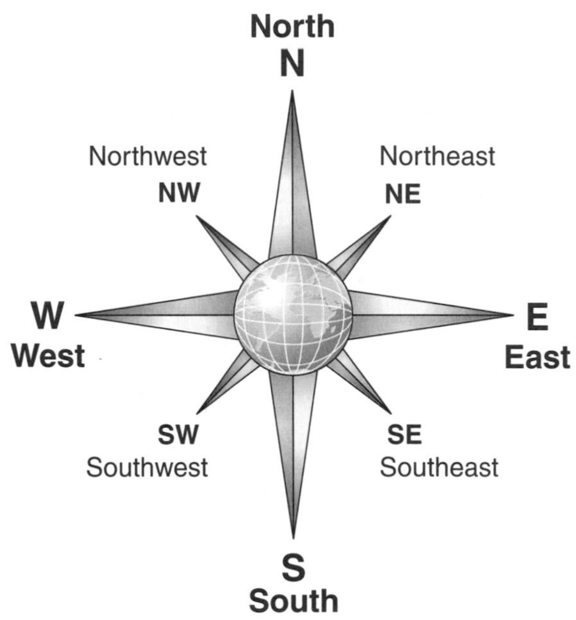

If you were trying to describe certain places or things in the United States, you might use a country map. A **country map** shows information about a country. It may show the boundary lines between countries and between states. It may show cities and roadways. A country map can also show the country's states or regions.

When you tell someone the location of a place on a country map, you may use different kinds of directions. **Cardinal directions** are the directions North, South, East, and West. Sometimes these directions are shortened to N for North, S for South, E for East, and W for West.

Intermediate directions are directions in between the cardinal directions. Northwest, Northeast, Southeast, and Southwest are intermediate directions.

The country map below shows regions of the United States. These regions are based on the location of the states in the United States. Cardinal and intermediate directions were used to name many of these regions.

Regions of the United States

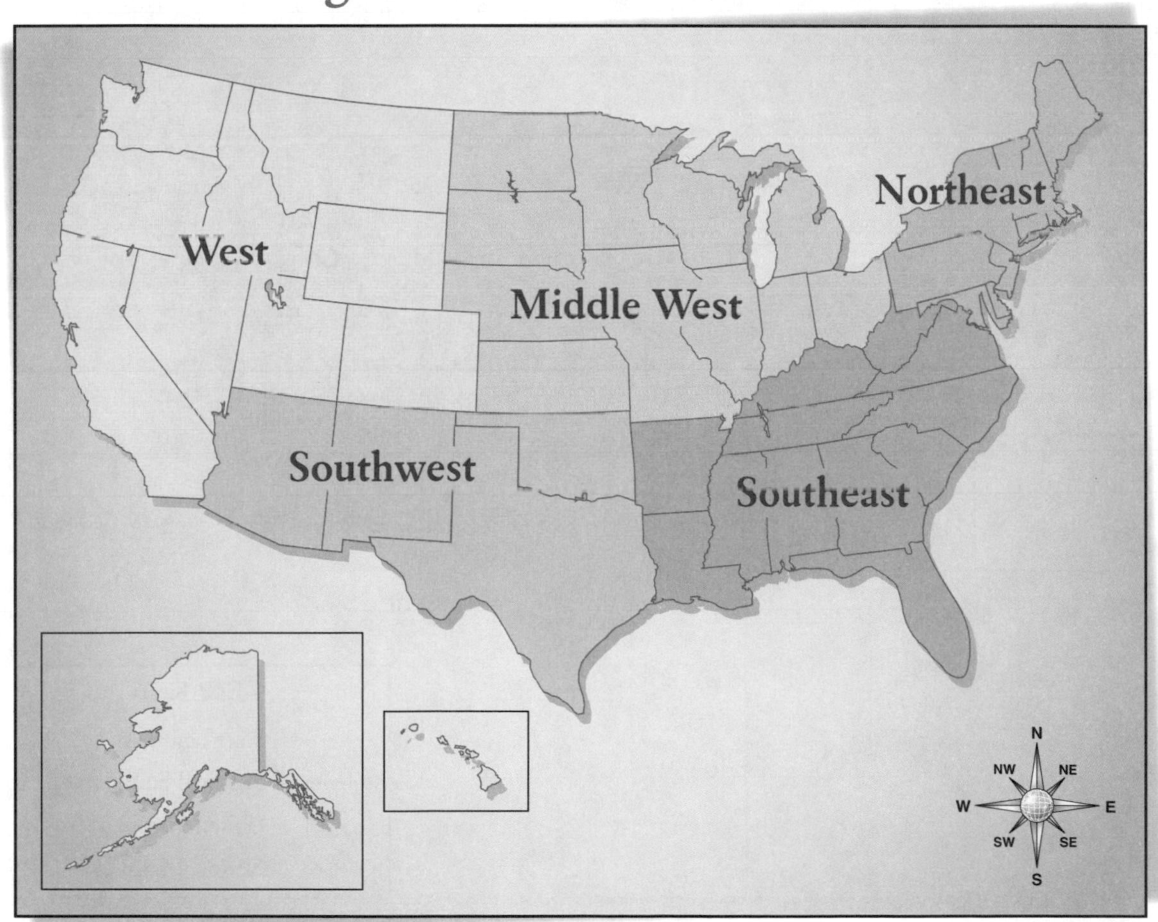

Look at the country map below. It shows the states in the United States and the countries that border to the north and south. The boundary between two countries is called a national boundary. The boundary between two states is called a state boundary.

Map of the United States

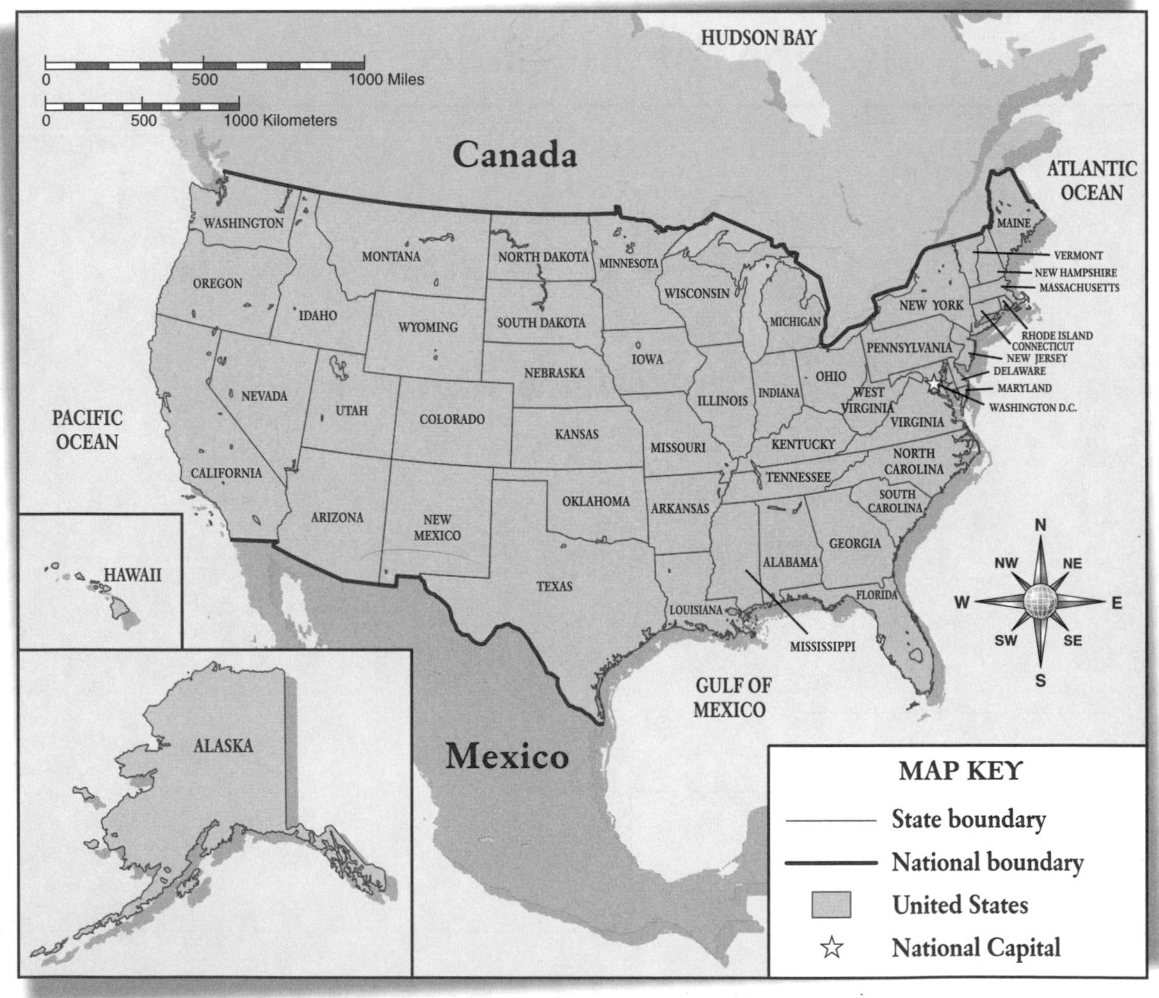

USE THIS SKILL

Read a Country Map

Use the country map on page 26 to answer these questions.

1. What country is to the north of the United States?
2. What state is on the west side of the Colorado boundary?
3. What ocean is to the west of the United States?
4. In what direction would you go to get to Nebraska from Texas?
5. Is South a cardinal or intermediate direction?
6. Imagine you are in Kentucky. Use an intermediate direction to describe in what direction you would go to get to Maine.

TEST TIP **You may be asked questions about a country map on a test. Read each question carefully and use the map to find the right answers.**

Skill 6

HOW TO

Read a Globe

Where in the World Are We?

To astronauts in outer space, planet Earth looks like a big blue marble with white swirls. The white swirls are really clouds, and the blue areas are oceans. As you get closer to Earth, land can also be seen.

Earth from outer space

To get a better picture of Earth, people make models of the way Earth looks from space. A **globe** is a model of Earth. It is round and shows many features of Earth. In order to see all of the features on the globe, you have to turn it. A globe is like a map on a ball.

Maps and globes are alike in some ways. Both a globe and map can show the whole world. Maps and globes are also different because a map is flat and a globe is round.

Globes show features of Earth's water and land. Globes show oceans and continents. Continents are large land areas on Earth. There are seven continents: North America, South America, Europe, Asia, Africa, Australia, and Antarctica.

Globes also show features such as the North and South Poles. The North Pole is the point farthest north on Earth. The South Pole is the point farthest south on Earth.

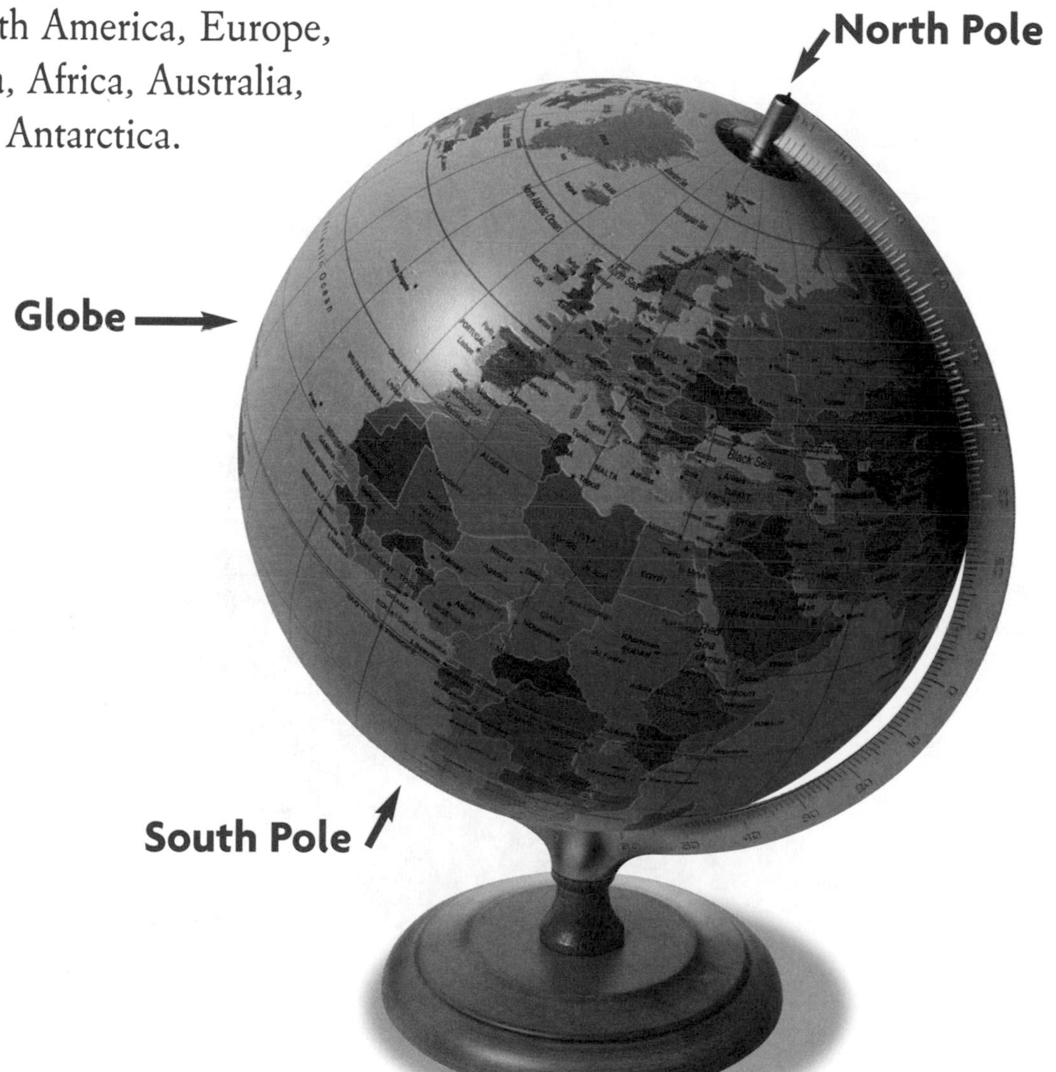

On a globe, there are lines that go around Earth. These are imaginary lines that help to tell where different places are on Earth's surface.

The **equator** is the line around the middle of Earth, halfway between the North and South Poles. Everything north of the equator is in the Northern Hemisphere. Everything south of the equator is in the Southern Hemisphere.

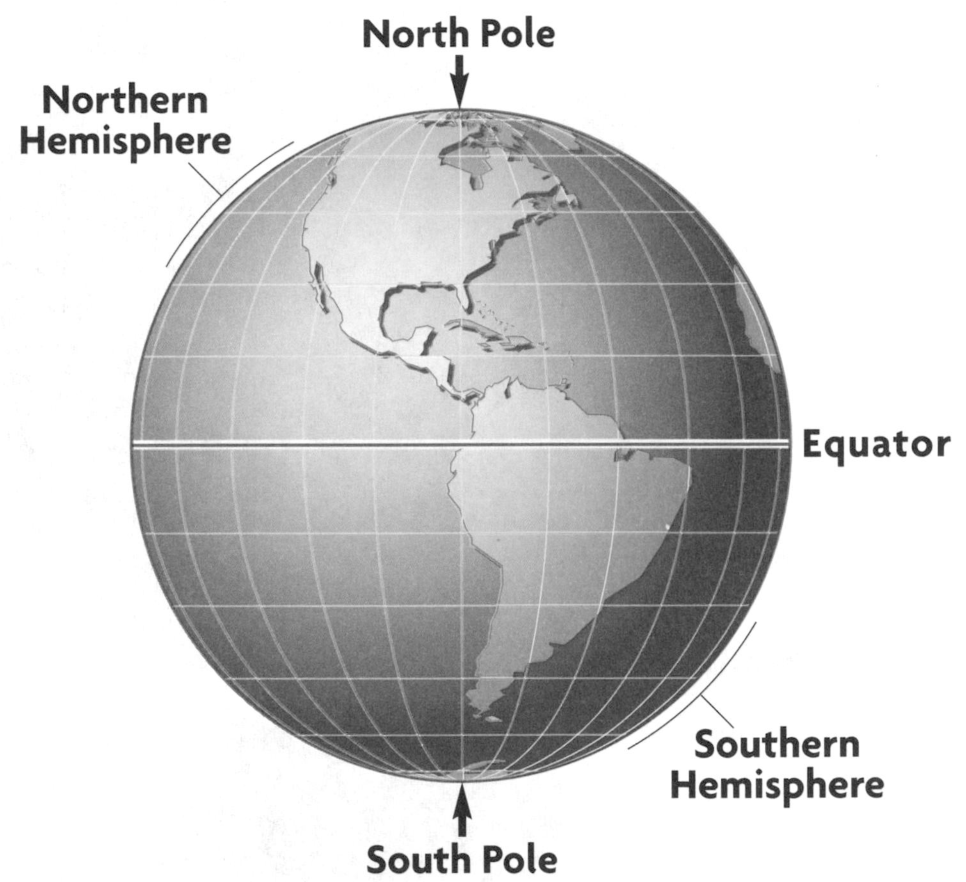

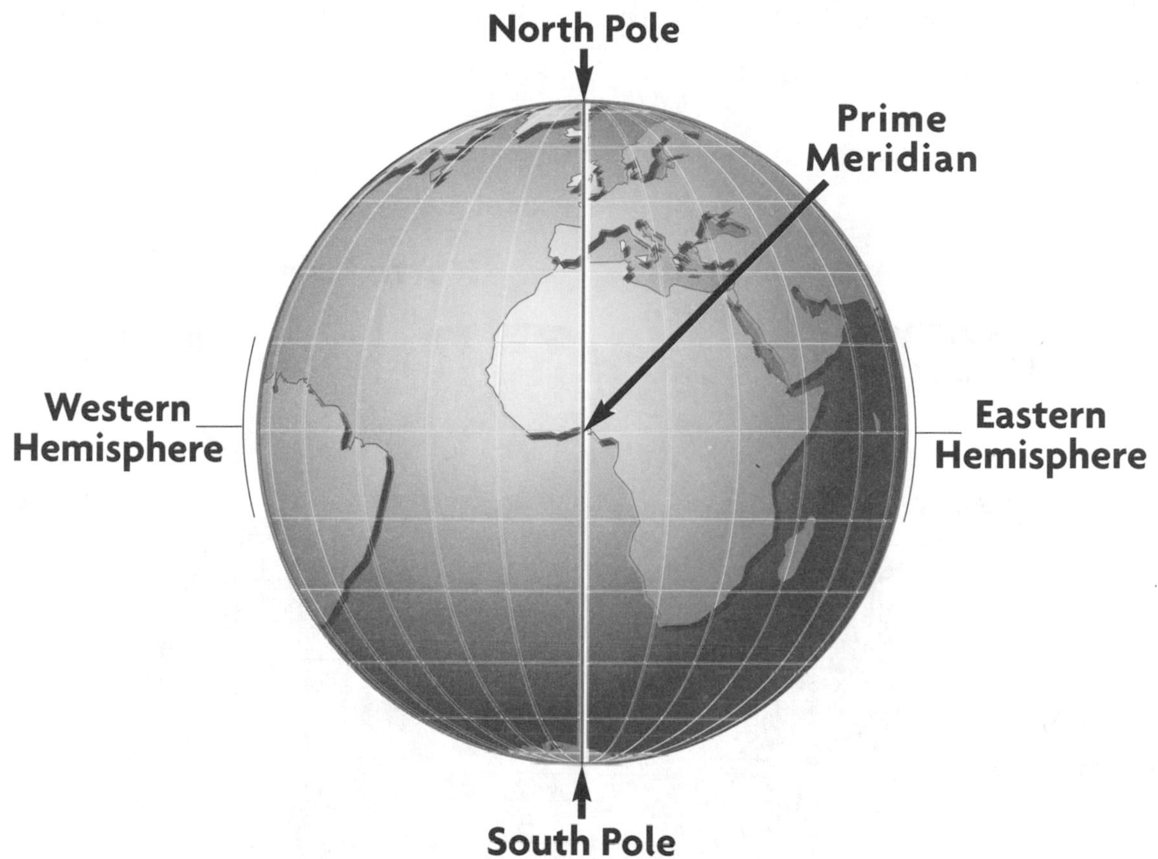

The **prime meridian** is the line that goes around Earth from the North Pole to the South Pole. Everything east of the prime meridian is in the Eastern Hemisphere. Everything west of the prime meridian is in the Western Hemisphere.

TIP To remember which hemisphere is which, turn the globe to Africa and think of a compass rose. The top half of the globe is in the Northern Hemisphere, the bottom half is in the Southern Hemisphere, Africa's western side is in the Western Hemisphere, and its eastern side is in the Eastern Hemisphere.

Look at the globe below. Think about what information the globe shows about Earth's water and land.

USE THIS SKILL

Read a Globe

Use the globe on page 32 to answer the following questions.

1. Is the United States in the Northern or the Southern Hemisphere?
2. On what continent is the United States?
3. Name two continents that the equator runs through.
4. Is the continent of Africa mostly in the Eastern or Western Hemisphere?
5. Is the continent of Antarctica closer to the North or the South Pole?
6. Name the imaginary line that divides Earth into a Northern Hemisphere and Southern Hemisphere.

TEST TIP

You may be asked about hemispheres on a test. Remember that the Northern Hemisphere includes all the area north of the equator, and the Southern Hemisphere includes all of the area south of the equator.

Skill 7

HOW TO

Read a Grid Map

Our Nation's Capital

Where can you see the Lincoln Memorial, the Washington Monument, and the Museum of Natural History all in one day? You could see these sites and more in our nation's capital, Washington, D.C.

If your class was visiting Washington, D.C., you might find sights to see on a grid map. A **grid map** is a map with lines that divide the map into smaller parts. The grid map on page 35 is divided into squares with lines forming columns and rows. Each column has a number and each row has a letter.

The grid map also has an index that lists places shown on the map and tells where each place can be found.

Find Lincoln Memorial in the index. Find B3 next to it. B3 is the square on the map where you can find the Lincoln Memorial. Find the letter B on the side of the map. Run your finger across the row until your finger is even with the number 3. Your finger is now on the square B3 where the Lincoln Memorial can be found.

Almost every city, town, and community has a grid map. It helps people find where things or places are located.

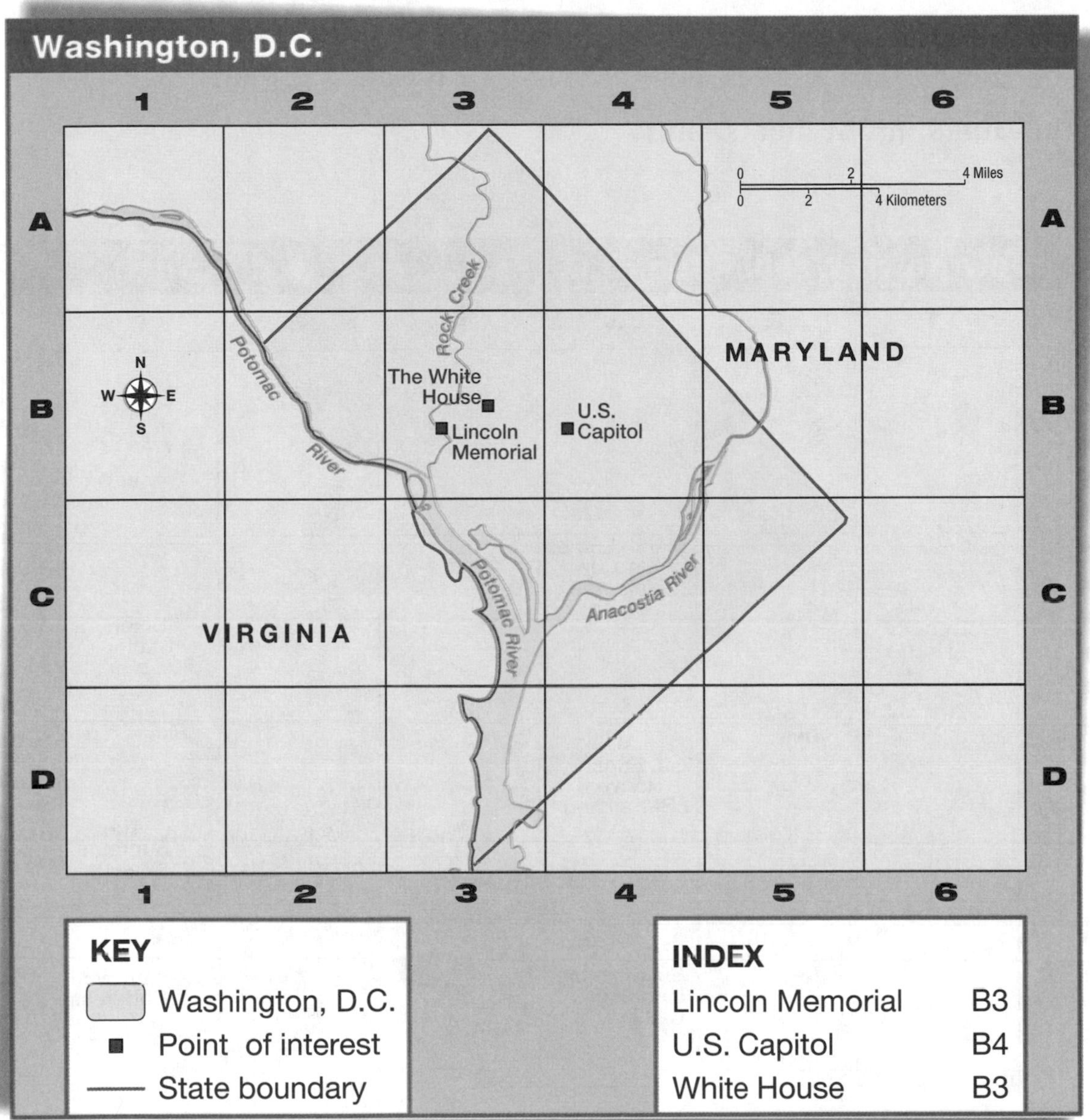

This grid map shows that Washington, D.C., is between the states of Maryland and Virginia on the Potomac River.

The first president of the United States, George Washington, chose this site for our nation's capital.

Look at the grid map below to see some of the government buildings, monuments, and museums that can be found in our nation's capital.

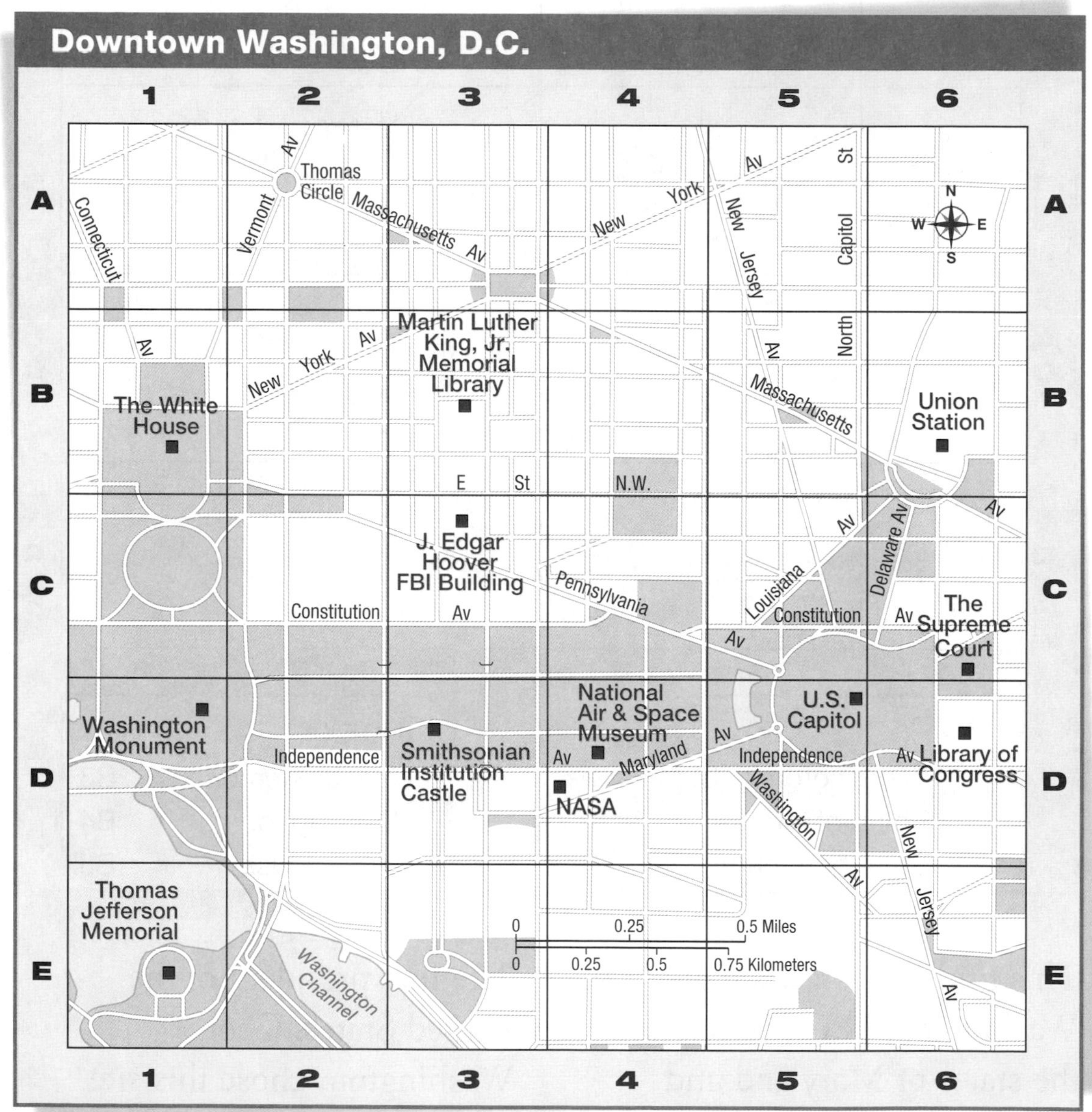

USE THIS SKILL

Read a Grid Map

Below is the index for the map on page 36. Use the grid map to fill in the blanks on the index.

INDEX

J. Edgar Hoover FBI Building	C3
Library of Congress	1.___
Martin Luther King, Jr. Memorial Library	B3
NASA	D4
National Air & Space Museum	D4
Smithsonian Institution Castle	2.___
Supreme Court	C6
Thomas Jefferson Memorial	3.___
4.________________________	B6
U.S. Capitol	5.___
6.________________________	D1
White House	7.___

TEST TIP **If you are asked to tell where a place or thing is on a grid map, always put the letter before the number—B3, not 3B.**

Skill 8

HOW TO

Read a Historical Map

Early America and the United States Today

A photo taken of you today would be different than a photo of you at ages one or five. By looking at both photos, you could see how you've changed over time. Photos record your own personal history.

Historical maps record the history of a country or an area. A **historical map** is a map that gives information about the past. Historical maps can show different kinds of information. The historical map below shows where the Pilgrims first landed in America.

First Landing of Pilgrims in America, November 1620

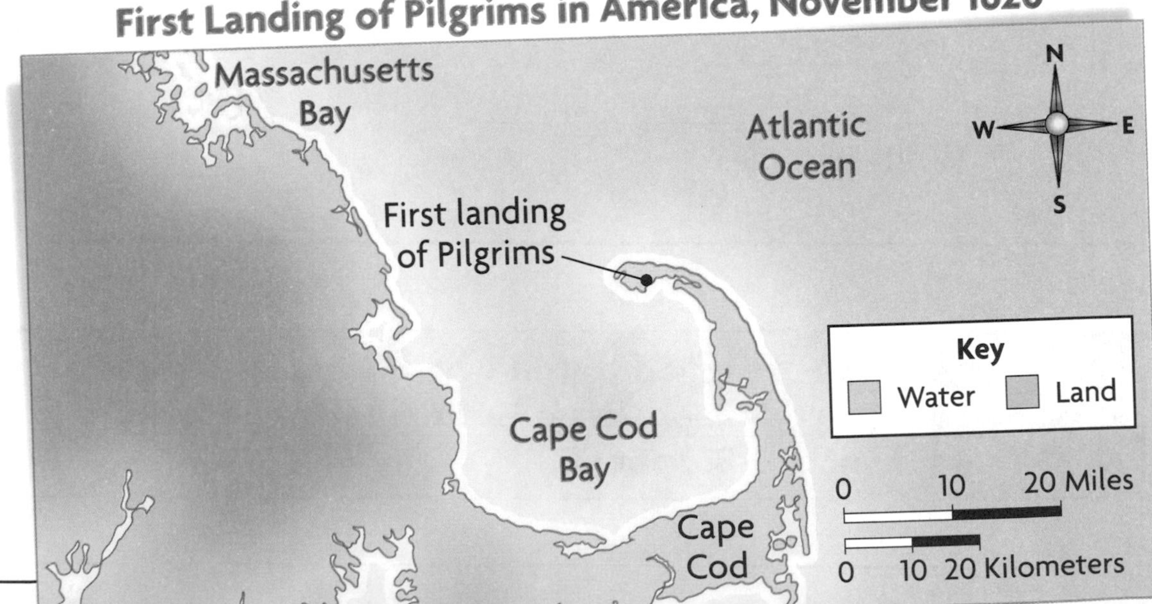

Route of Pilgrims to America, 1620

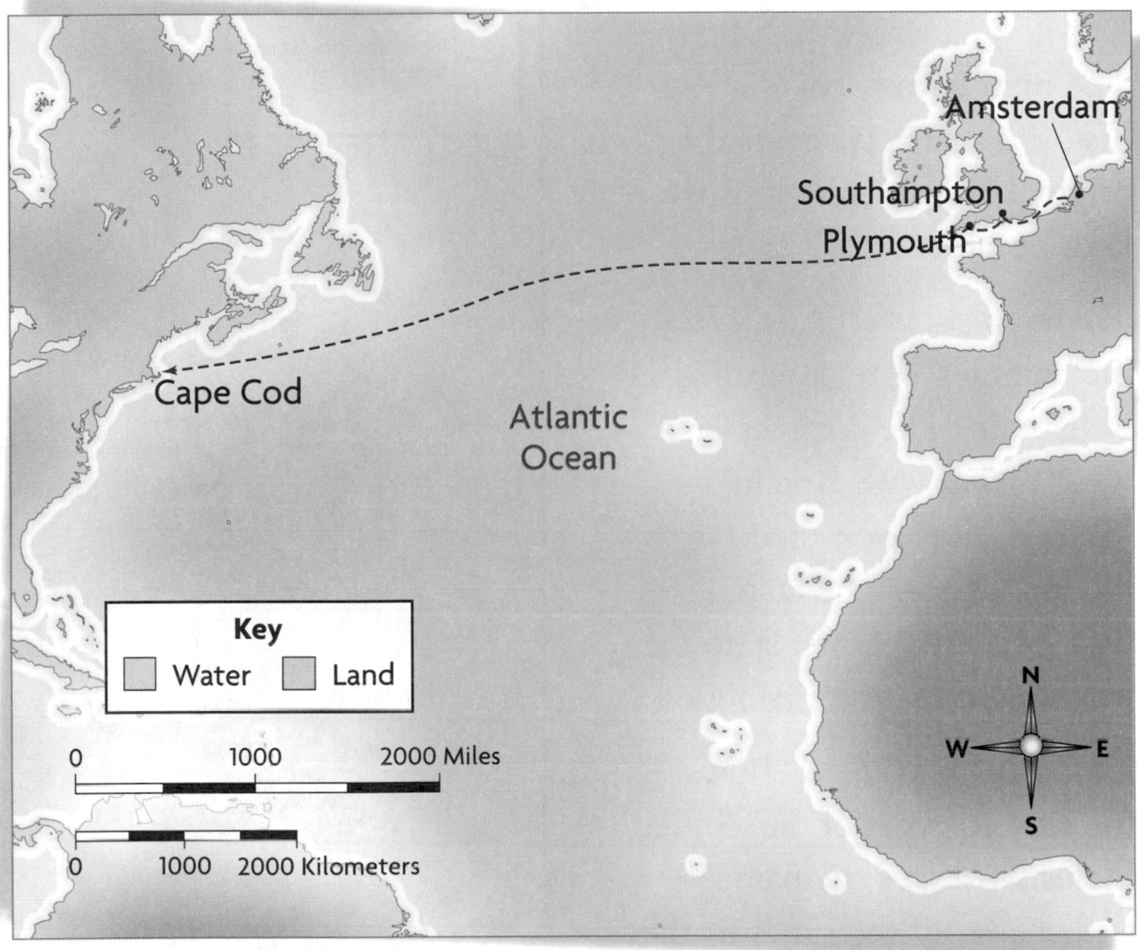

When you read a historical map, look at the map title and the map key. The title will tell you the name of the place and the time period shown on the map. The map key shows other information, such as what the colors on the map stand for.

The title of the map above tells that the Pilgrims traveled to America in the year 1620. The map key above shows that blue areas along the travel route between Amsterdam and Cape Cod are water and the green areas are land.

The map on this page is a historical map. It shows the original British colonies that later became today's states.

The map shows that in 1763 the colonies were controlled by Britain. The colonies later went to war with Britain. In 1776, they won their independence. The colonies then became the first states of the United States of America.

The map on page 41 shows the eastern coast of the United States. It shows the names and shapes of the states as they appear on a U.S. map today.

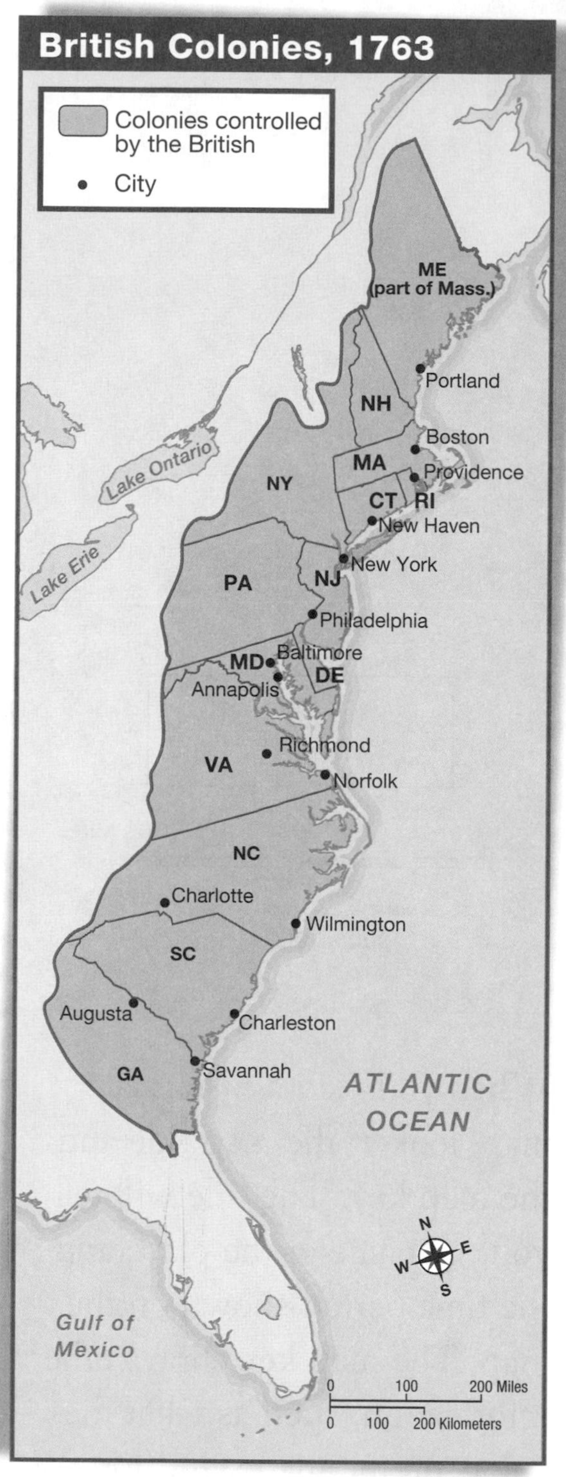

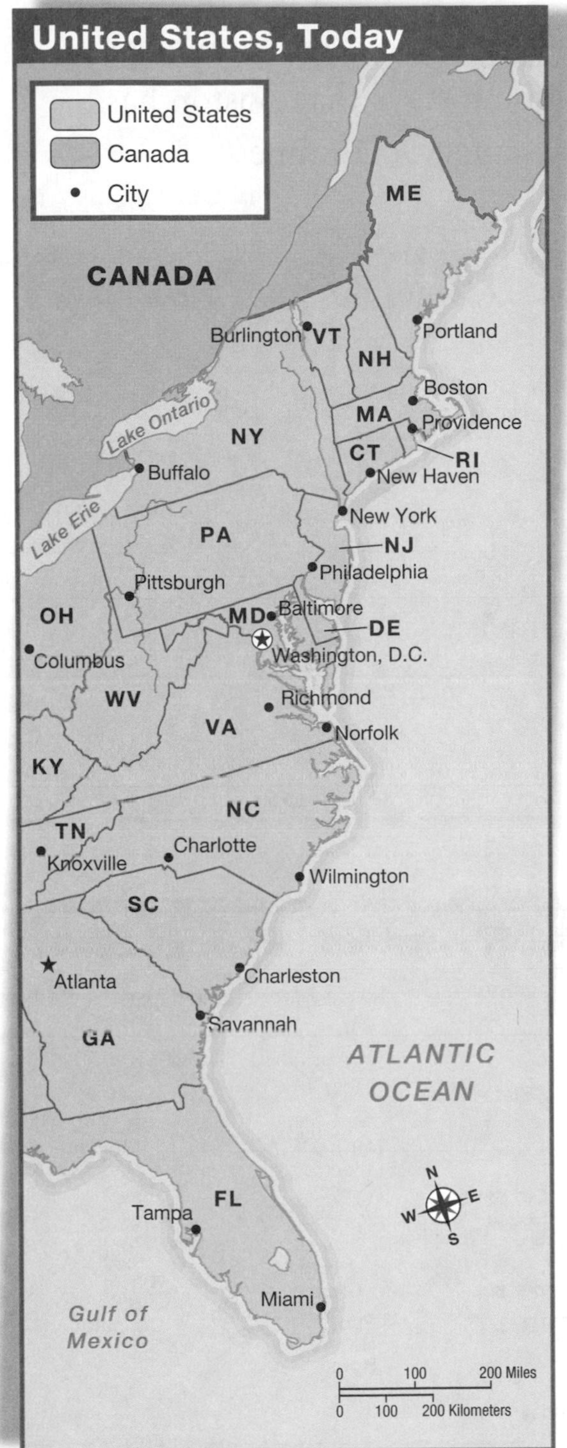

When you read a historical map, try to compare it to a current map showing the same area. By comparing what you see on the different maps, you can see how the area has changed over time.

By comparing the maps on pages 40 and 41, you can see how the United States has changed over time. You can see that some of the states look different than they did when they were colonies. The colony boundaries changed and became state boundaries as the area changed over time. You can also see that the names of the 13 colonies and states are similar on both maps. Some of the cities shown on the maps are also similar.

Look at the maps below. Compare the historical map with the current map of Boston. Think about how the maps show ways that Boston has changed over time.

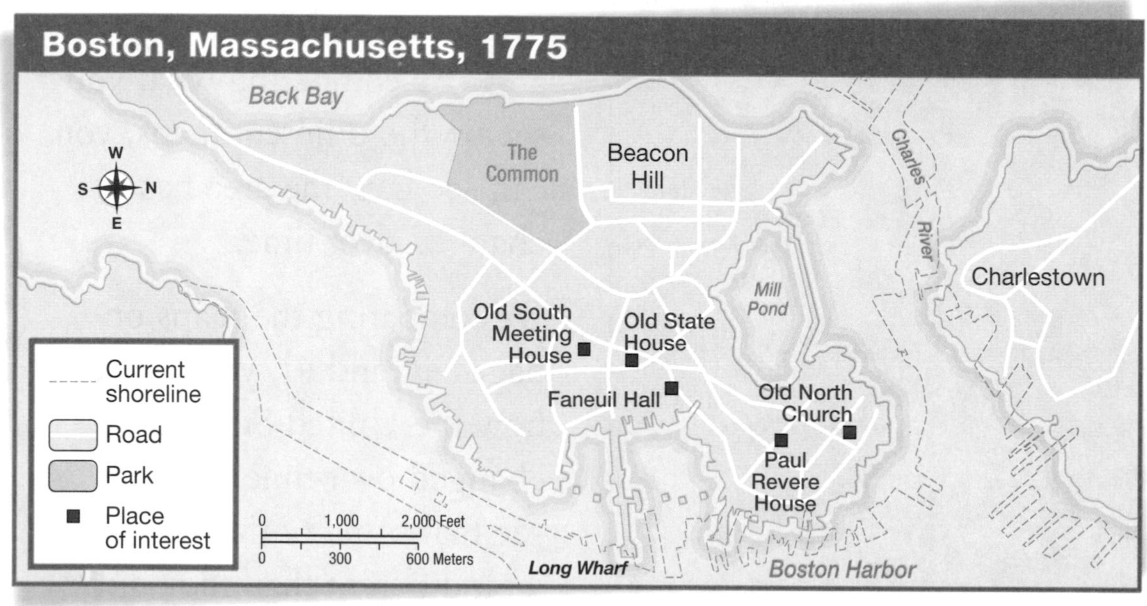

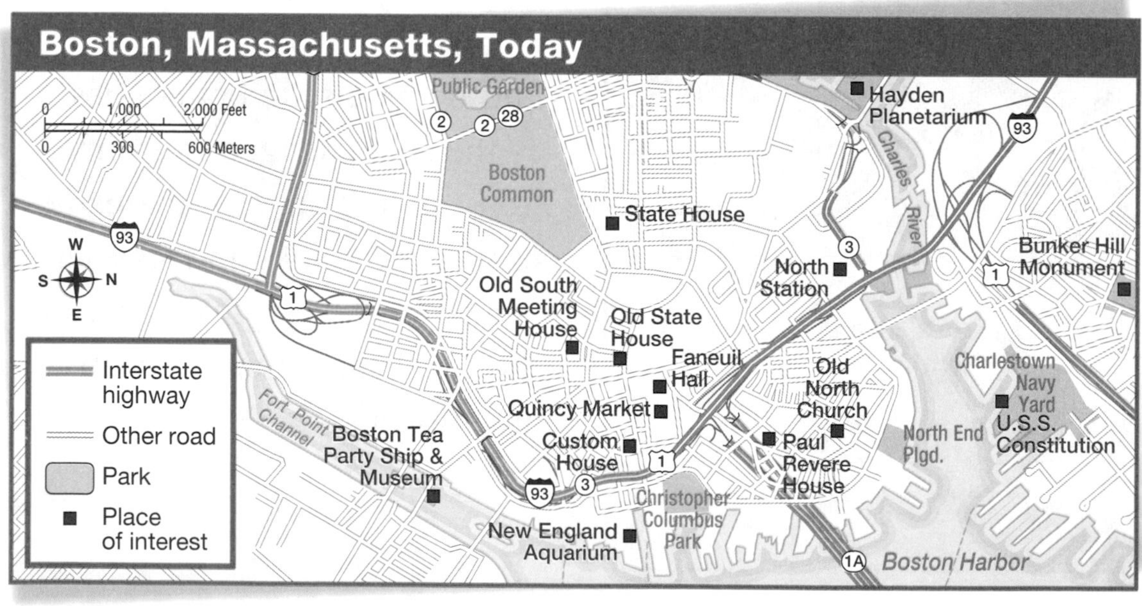

USE THIS SKILL

Read a Historical Map

Use the maps on page 42 to answer the questions.

1. Which map on page 42 is the historical map? Why?
2. What period of time is shown on the historical map of Boston?
3. Name two things that are the same about the two maps.
4. Name two things that are different about the two maps.
5. If you were writing a report about the places to see in the city of Boston today, which map would you use?
6. If you were writing a report about life in early American cities, which map would you use?

TEST TIP

You may be asked to read a historical map on a test. Before answering a question, look carefully at the map. It may be very different from the way things are today.

Skill 9

HOW TO

Read a Cultural Map

Native American Lands

If you drew a map showing where every member of a family lives—all the aunts, uncles, grandparents, and cousins—you would have a special kind of map. Your map would show the location of one group of people who share something in common.

Families are one type of group. A group of people who share things in common sometimes live in the same area. Groups of Native Americans have lived together in areas across the United States. A Native American group, like other groups, has its own culture.

Culture is a group of people's way of life. The language, religion, clothing, and the music shared by a group of people are all part of its culture. A **cultural map** shows where people sharing the same culture live or lived.

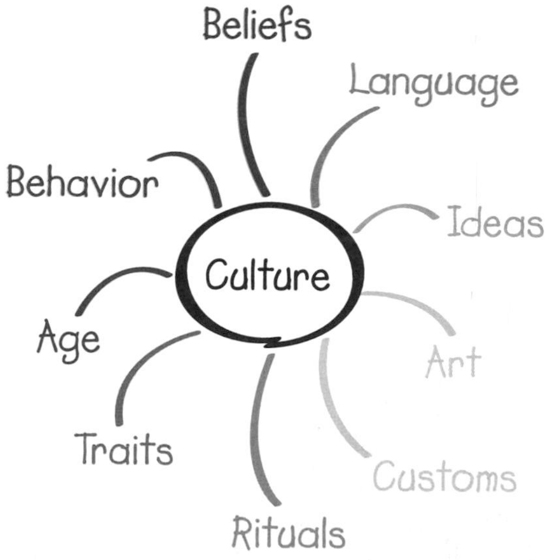

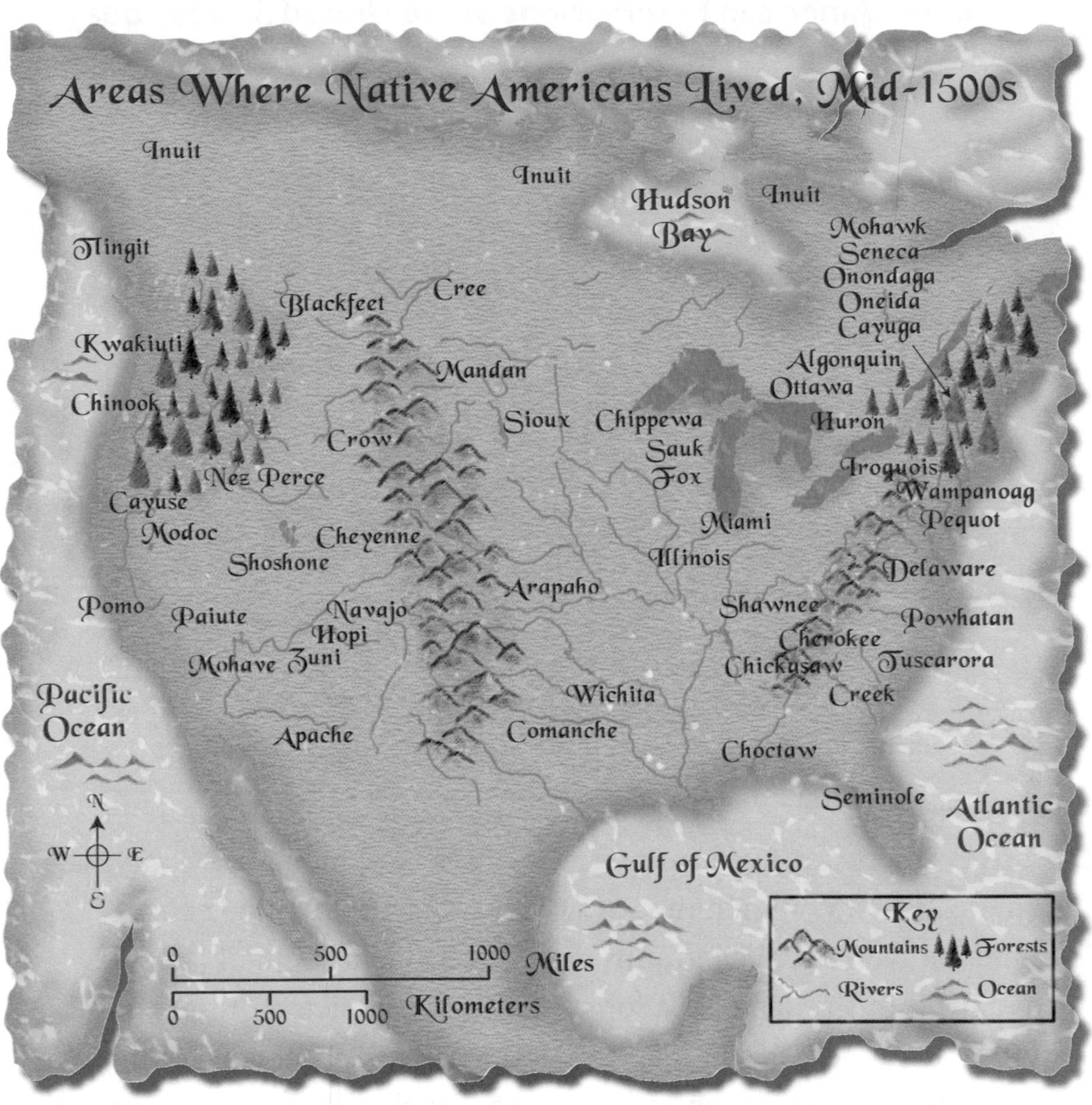

The cultural map above shows different areas in North America where Native American groups made their homes.

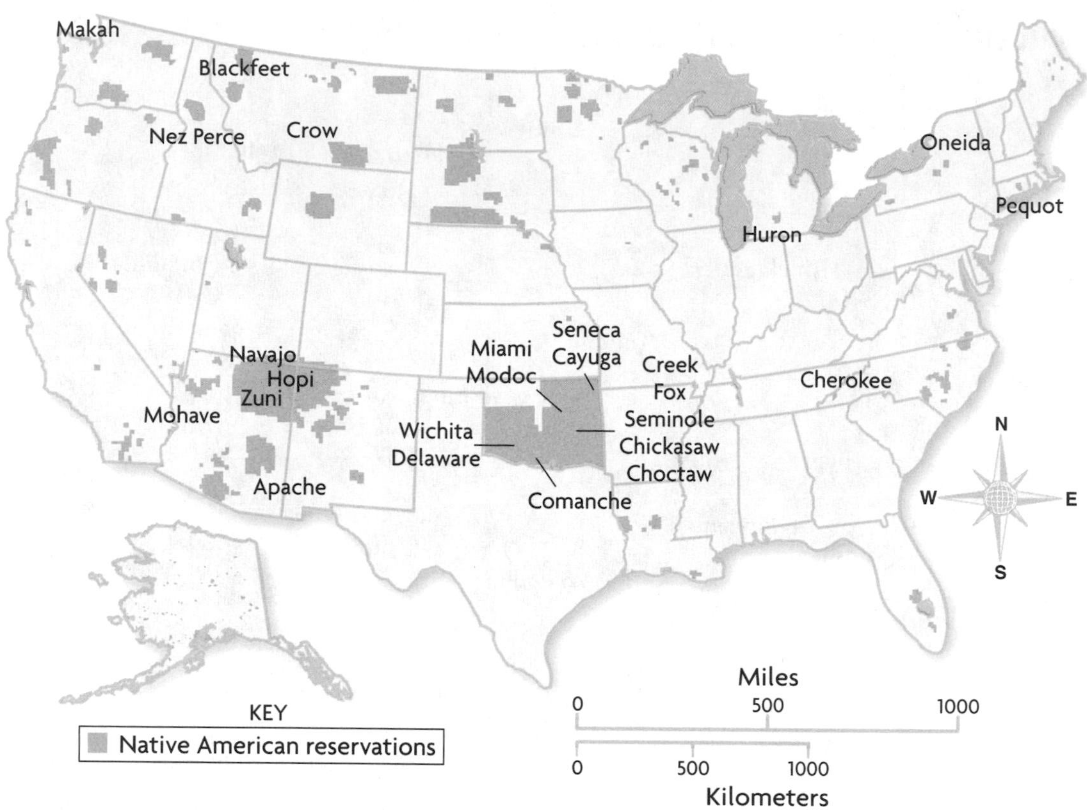

Native Americans lived in America's first communities. Some Native American groups have lived in the same area for thousands of years. The map above shows the location of some Native American lands, called reservations, in the United States today.

A reservation is tribal land that is protected by the U.S. government. Some Native Americans live on reservations and others do not. A group's reservation is often an important part of its culture because it is a place where tribal dances, music, religion, and customs are shared.

The Cherokee Nation is one of the largest Native American groups in the United States. After 1800, the Cherokee formed their own tribal government. An important part of the Cherokee culture is the traditional Stomp Dance and sacred dance site.

Cherokee Stomp Dance

At the tip of Washington state, you can find the Makah Nation. The Makah celebrate their culture during Makah Days with canoe races, traditional games, dancing, singing, and a parade. The Makah have hunted and fished in the Pacific Ocean for thousands of years.

Makah elder teaching children on the beach

Look at the cultural map below. Think about what the map tells about the Native American groups shown on the map.

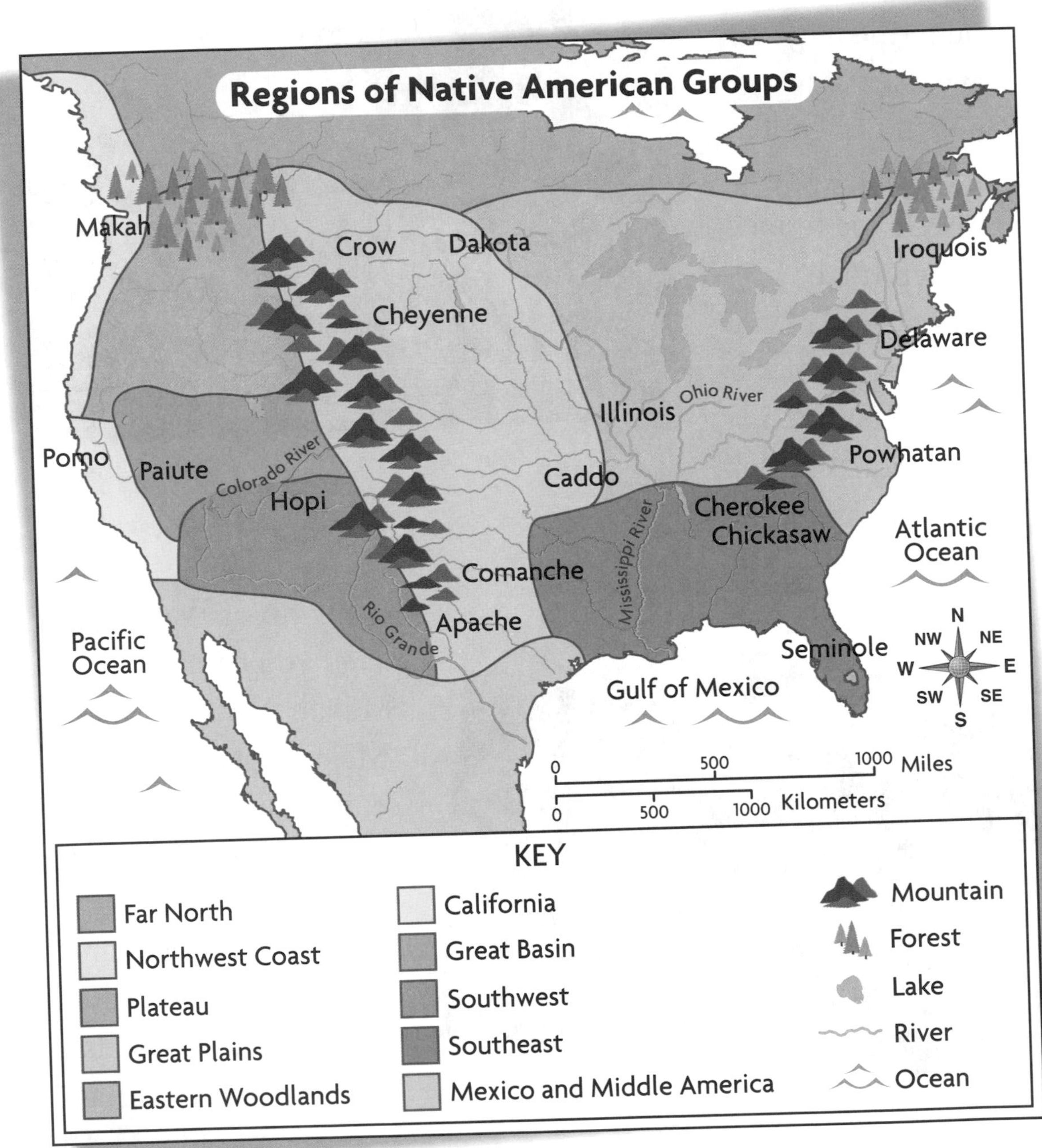

USE THIS SKILL

Read a Cultural Map

Use the map on page 48 to answer these questions.

1. Which river might have helped Native Americans in the southeast region travel north and south?
2. In what region is the Cheyenne group shown on the map?
3. Name two regions on the map that have forests.
4. What river might the Hopi have used for travel or for fishing?
5. Name two Native American groups that can be found in regions along the Pacific Ocean.

TEST TIP

When a test asks questions about a cultural map, take time to study the map legend. The symbols and colors will help you answer the questions.

Skill 10

HOW TO

Read a Road Map

Mountain Highway

Did you know that there are mountains that look blue from a distance? The Cherokee called these mountains "the Blue Wall." You can visit these mountains by traveling on a mountain road that goes along for over 400 miles!

The Blue Ridge Mountains

The Blue Ridge is a mountain range that goes from Pennsylvania to Georgia. The road that follows the ridges of these mountains is called the Blue Ridge Parkway. It is about 469 miles long and goes through the states of Virginia and North Carolina.

The Blue Ridge Parkway runs between Shenandoah National Park in Virginia and Great Smoky Mountains National Park in North Carolina. Along the Parkway there are hiking trails, waterfalls, and places to camp. There are also farms and folk art centers where people can learn about the early settlers.

You can learn about the Blue Ridge Parkway by looking at a road map. A **road map** is a map that shows the roads in an area. Road maps can help you plan a trip or see how to get from one place to another. Road maps may show small roads, state highways, and interstate highways. They may also show places to visit like state and national parks.

The road map below shows some of the interstate highways in the United States. Interstate highways are large roads that cross more than one state. The map also shows the Blue Ridge Parkway. You can see how all the roads on the map cross state boundaries.

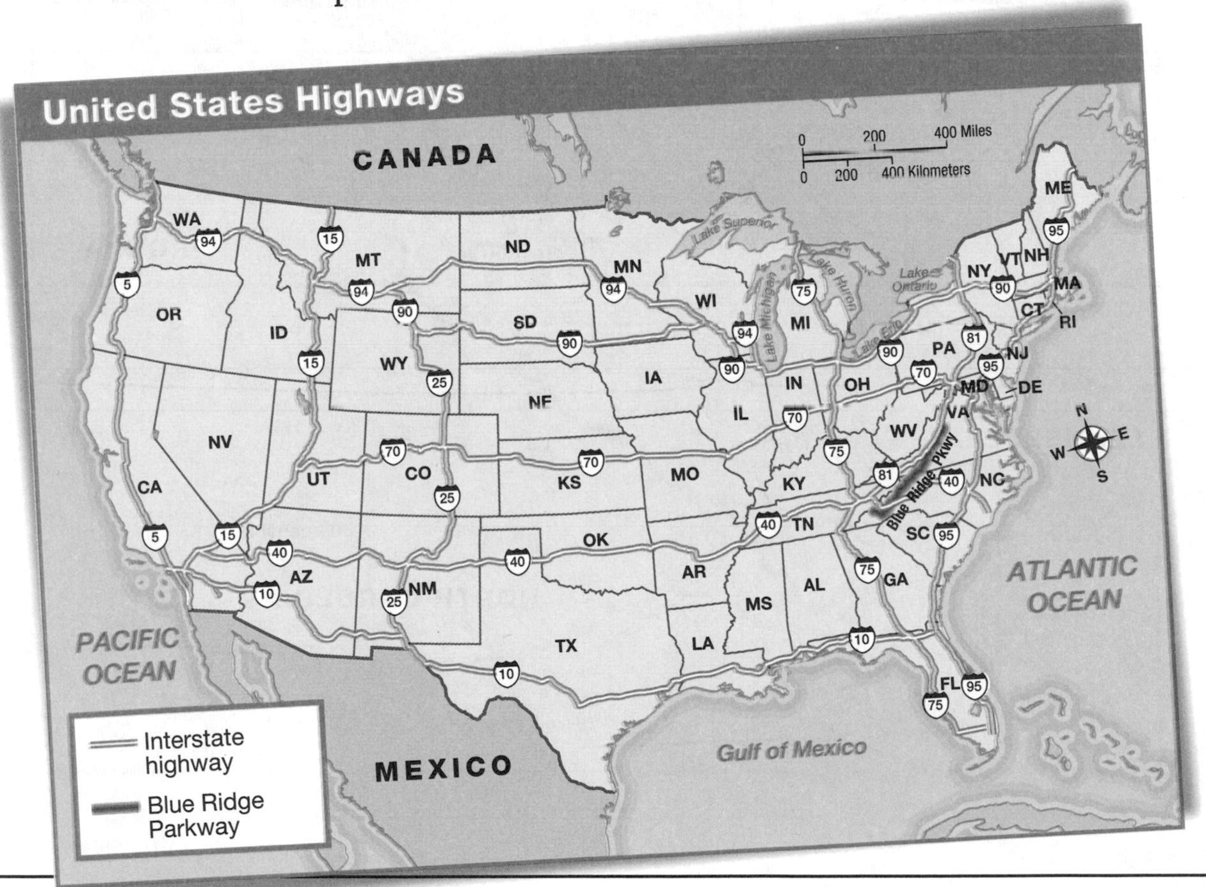

The road map below shows some interstate highways, national parks, and national forests that can be found along the Blue Ridge Parkway.

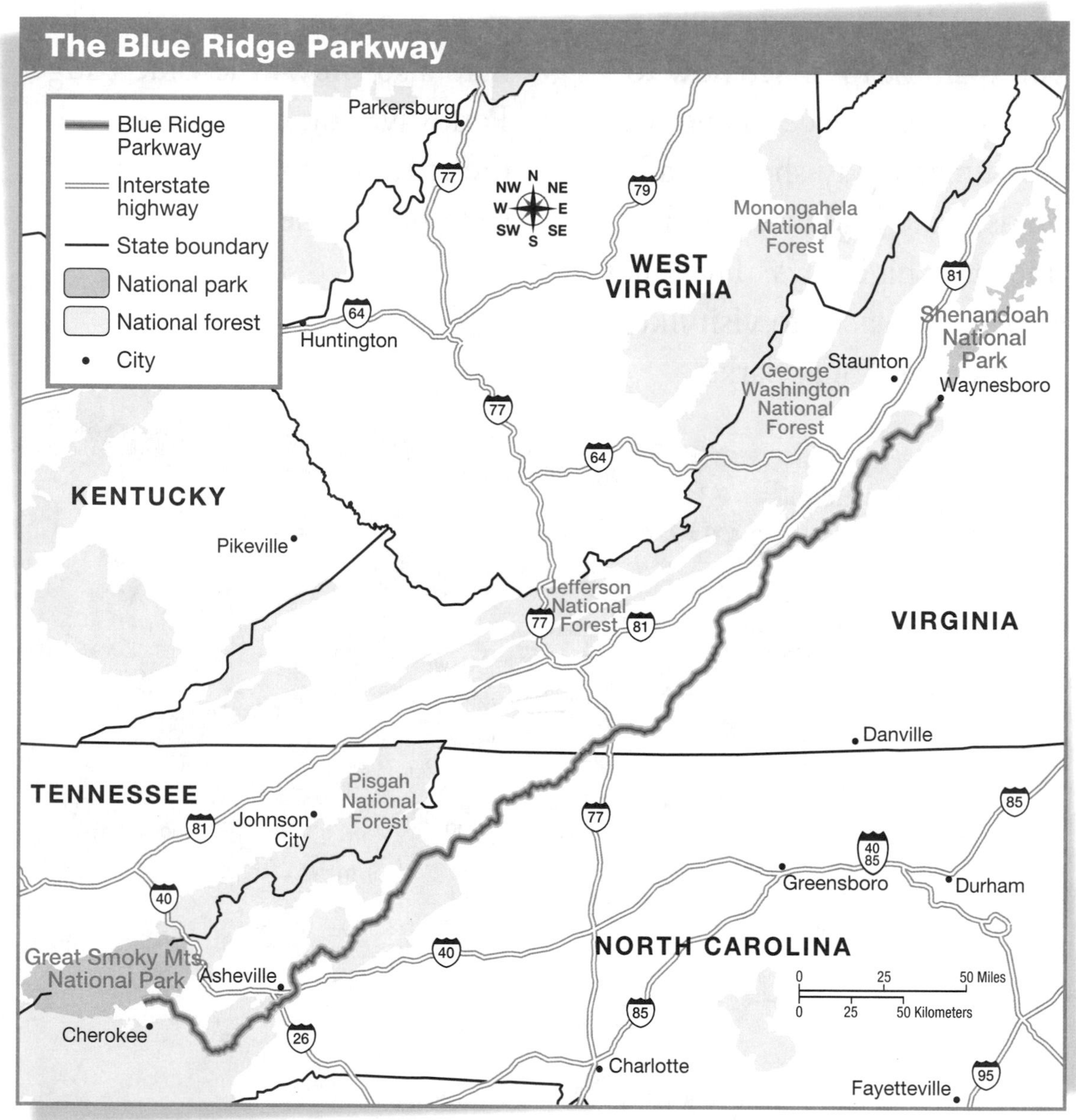

USE THIS SKILL

Read a Road Map

Use the map of the Blue Ridge Parkway on page 52 to answer these questions.

1. If you were in Waynesboro, Virginia, in which direction would you travel on the Blue Ridge Parkway to get to Asheville, North Carolina?
2. About how many miles is Pikeville, Kentucky, from the Blue Ridge Parkway?
3. Name two national forests that are located west of the Parkway.
4. On what roads would you drive to get to the Parkway from Huntington, West Virginia?
5. In what state does Interstate 40 cross the Blue Ridge Parkway?

TEST TIP

On a test, you may need to read a road map. Look at only the road that will help you find the answer to the question. Don't pay attention to other roads shown on the map.

Reading and Thinking Skills

Skill 11

HOW TO

Classify

Having a Good Time in Georgia!

Did you know that the state of Georgia was one of the original thirteen colonies? Georgia has an interesting history as well as an exciting future.

A good way to learn about events that happened in Georgia is to classify them. When you **classify,** you put things into groups. When studying history, you can put events into groups of time.

You can classify events as past, present, or future. Past events happened before today. Present events are happening now. Future events will happen sometime after today. Can you find information about the past, present, and future in the following reading?

In 1950, over three million people lived in Georgia. Georgia's population today is about eight million. By the year 2010, about eight and a half million people will likely live in Georgia.

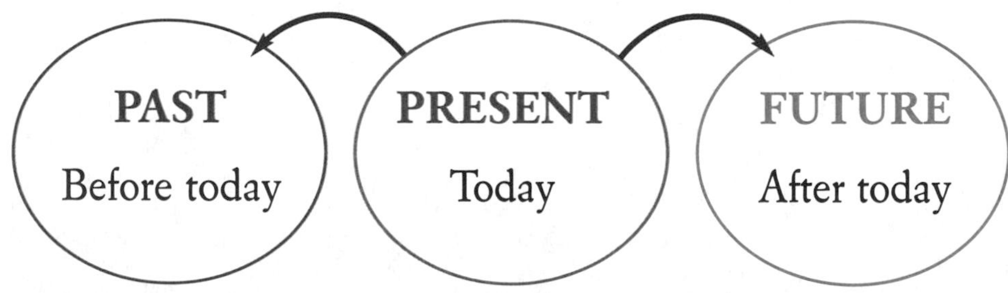

STEPS IN Classifying

Use these steps to classify information.

TIP When classifying events as past, present, and future, look for words like **yesterday, today,** and **tomorrow.**

1 Study the Information

Look at the information you have. Think about how things are alike and different. Find details that you could use to compare and contrast each thing or event.

2 Sort into Groups

Make two or more groups that show how some of the things or events are alike. Use the details of each thing or event to put it into a group.

Georgia's Population

Present
About eight million people today

Past
Over three million people in 1950

Future
About eight and a half million people in 2010

Groups Based on Time

EXAMPLE OF Classifying

As you read this story, think about what information you can classify as past, present, and future.

Traveling in Georgia

There is a lot of traveling going on in Georgia. People go to work and school. People go to grocery stores, museums, and movies. People also travel from one city to another. How do they get there?

Past → In the past, people walked, rode on a horse, or traveled by boat. In the 1830s and 1840s, railroads became a popular way to travel from one city to another.

Present → Trains are still used today. In Georgia, a high-speed train system with 20 stations is being built to connect many cities in Georgia. In the future, it will have 40 stations and travel to even more cities. **← Future**

USE THIS SKILL

Classify

Classify the information in the questions below as past, present, or future.

1. In 1996, the Summer Olympic Games were held in Atlanta, Georgia.

   A. Past B. Present C. Future

2. Today's weather in Georgia is fair.

   A. Past B. Present C. Future

3. The Coca-Cola Space Science Center in Columbus, Georgia, now has a space mission learning center, laser concerts, and an observatory with a research telescope.

   A. Past B. Present C. Future

4. Next week you could be part of a puppet-making workshop at the Center for Puppetry Arts in Atlanta, Georgia.

   A. Past B. Present C. Future

TEST TIP

On a test, look for words like a long time ago, now, and in the future to help you classify information as past, present, or future.

Skill 12

HOW TO

Compare and Contrast

At Home with the Pueblo and Dakota

Think about Native American children living more than 100 years ago. Do you think they liked to play and laugh like you do now? Of course they did! Do you think they listened to the same music as you do? Probably not.

A good way to learn about people, places, or things is to compare and contrast them. When you **compare,** you tell how the people, places, or things are alike. When you **contrast,** you tell how they are different.

Can you tell what is alike and different in the story below?

There were no schools for Pueblo and Dakota children. Young people learned by helping their parents.

The Pueblo grew corn for food. Young girls learned to crush the grain and cook it. Pueblo boys were taught how to plant it.

The Dakota hunted buffalo for food. Dakota boys learned to shoot arrows at a young age. The girls were taught to make buffalo skin clothing.

STEPS IN **Comparing and Contrasting**

Use these steps to compare and contrast.

1 Identify the Topics

Think about the topics you want to compare and contrast. Topics are the people, places, or things that you read, write, or tell about.

Pueblo and Dakota

Same

1. No schools
2. Parents taught children.

Different

1. Pueblo grew corn for food.
2. Dakota hunted buffalo for food.

2 List Similarities

Write down ways that the topics are the same.

3 List Differences

Write down ways that the topics are different.

TIP You can make a chart to help you compare and contrast pictures and descriptions.

EXAMPLE OF **Comparing and Contrasting**

As you read this story, think about how Dakota and Pueblo homes were both alike and different.

Home Is Where the Heart Is

Alike

Early Native Americans built homes for shelter and comfort just like we do today. Both Dakota and Pueblo homes were cool in summer and warm in winter. But the homes of these two Native American groups looked very different.

The Dakota lived on the Great Plains. They moved a lot to hunt buffalo. This means they needed a home that could move with them. The tepee was the perfect answer. It was a cone-shaped tent made by covering long poles with buffalo hides. A tepee could be put up by two women in an hour. It was fast and easy.

Different

Different

The Pueblo lived in the Southwest. They did not move around often. They built very strong houses. Many were made with sun-dried clay bricks called adobe. The dried adobe was hard and waterproof. Some houses were built of stone. They took a long time to build and some still stand today.

USE THIS SKILL

Compare and Contrast

Look at the two pictures below. List two ways the pictures are alike and different.

Dakota tepee

Pueblo adobe house

TEST TIP

When you compare and contrast on a test, think about similarities and differences. Compare the answer choices to the information in the reading passage.

Skill 13

HOW TO

Determine Cause and Effect

Gold, Sweet Gold?

"In California, the rivers are full of gold." Promises of gold caused many people to move to California during the Gold Rush. But getting rich wasn't very easy.

Why did people move to California? What happened when they got there? When you look for reasons why things happen, you are looking for causes and effects. A **cause** is the reason why something happens. The **effect** is what happens.

CAUSE

January 1848

EXTRA! EXTRA!

Gold found in California!

A carpenter named James Marshall found gold when building a mill for John Sutter. He wasn't even looking for gold, and now he's a rich man!

Newspaper articles tell about gold in California.

STEPS IN Determining Cause and Effect

You can use these steps to find causes and effects.

1 What Happened?

First ask yourself what happened. This will help you find the effect.

2 Why Did It Happen?

Then ask yourself why this happened. This is the cause.

3 Which Came First?

Think about the cause and effect. Then ask yourself which came first. The cause makes the effect happen. The cause comes before the effect.

EFFECT

Many people moved to California to find gold.

EXAMPLE OF **Determining Cause and Effect**

Read the text below and look for causes and effects.

Many people never found gold in California. Some people became very poor **← Effect** because they spent most of their savings on the supplies they needed to mine for gold. **(Cause →)** The trip to California, food, and tools were very expensive. Some people became very sad **(Effect →)** because they didn't have enough money to travel back to their homes and families. **← Cause** They had spent their money and never found gold.

Why?	What happened?
Cause	Effect
They spent most of their savings on the supplies they needed to mine for gold.	Some people became very poor.
This came first.	**This came later.**
Cause	Effect
They didn't have enough money to travel back to their homes and families.	Some people became very sad.
This came first.	**This came later.**

USE THIS SKILL

Determine Cause and Effect

Read each passage to find the cause or the effect.

In 1848, there were about 1,000 people living in San Francisco, California. Because many people moved to California to find gold, around 35,000 people lived in San Francisco by 1850.

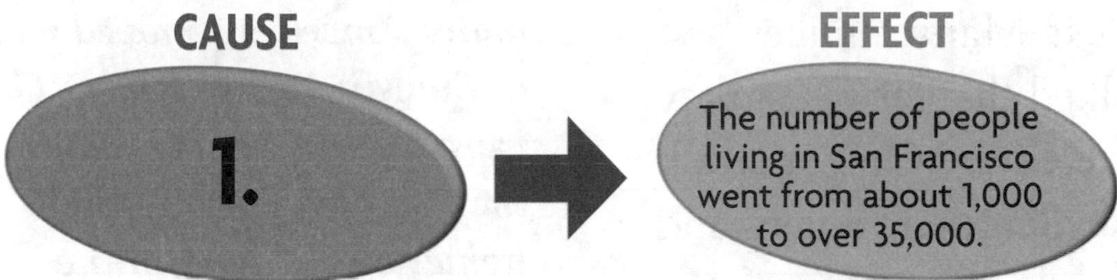

People from all over the world—China, Mexico, Germany, France, Ireland, and other countries—came to California because they thought they could find gold.

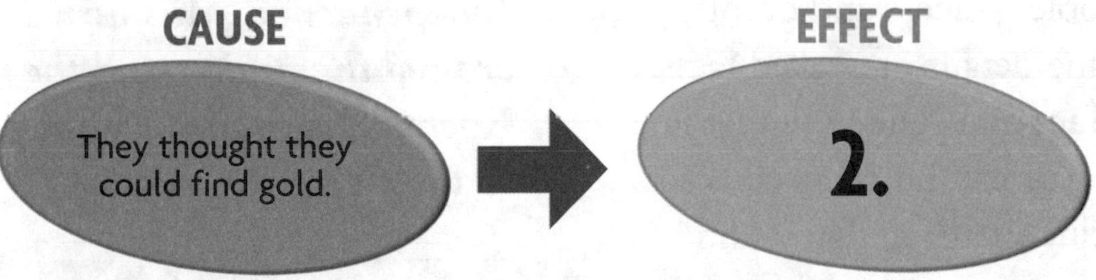

TEST TIP	**On a test, you may be asked to find causes and effects. Look for something that happened to find the effect. Look for the reason why something happened to find the cause.**

Skill 14

HOW TO

Tell Fact from Opinion

On the Oregon Trail

Could you walk 2,000 miles? Many families walked this far when they traveled the Oregon Trail. They left their homes and moved west looking for a better life.

When you read about history, you can learn details about people, places, and events. Some details are called facts. A **fact** is a statement that is true. It can be checked. Facts include names, dates, and places. Look for the facts in the following reading.

Beginning in the 1840s, many Americans moved west of the Mississippi River. They were called settlers because they wanted to settle their homes on the land in the west. Many settlers followed the same paths. One path was called the Oregon Trail. The Oregon Trail started in Independence, Missouri. It crossed the prairie and the Rocky Mountains, leading to the Oregon Territory.

Fact: Beginning in the 1840s, many settlers moved west.

Fact: The Oregon Trail started in Missouri.

Some details may also be given as opinions. An **opinion** is a statement telling what a person thinks, believes, or feels. Opinions are different from facts. You cannot prove an opinion. Look at these opinions from travelers on the Oregon Trail. Think about how the opinions about the Oregon Trail are different from the facts.

Opinion: "Settlers should travel in large groups."

Opinion: "Life in Oregon will be better than life in Indiana."

On the Oregon Trail

STEPS IN Telling Fact from Opinion

Facts and opinions can help you learn what life was like on the Oregon Trail. Use these steps to tell facts from opinions.

A family with its covered wagons

1 Find the Facts

Numbers and names of places can help you find facts. Numbers can lead you to key facts.

Beginning in the 1840s, many settlers moved west.

Names of places can help you find facts.

The Oregon Trail started in Missouri.

2 Find the Opinions

Certain words can help you find opinions. Opinions often contain words such as *better, best, worst, more, most, always, never, seems,* and *should.*

The trail seems to go on forever.

Settlers should travel in large groups.

3 List Facts and Opinions

When you read, you may find both facts and opinions. You can list the facts and opinions in a chart. Think about how they are alike and different.

TIPS

- **Facts can be proven.**
- **Opinions tell the thoughts or feelings of the writer.**

Life on the Oregon Trail

Facts	Opinions
The travelers walked 15 to 20 miles each day.	It was better to go over the mountains than to go around them.
Settlers floated their wagons across the Snake River.	The trail was beautiful and peaceful.
Many people became sick and died during the trip.	The dark night sky was always frightening.

EXAMPLE OF Telling Fact from Opinion

Some people who traveled on the Oregon Trail wrote diaries. Think about the difference between facts and opinions as you read the diary entry below.

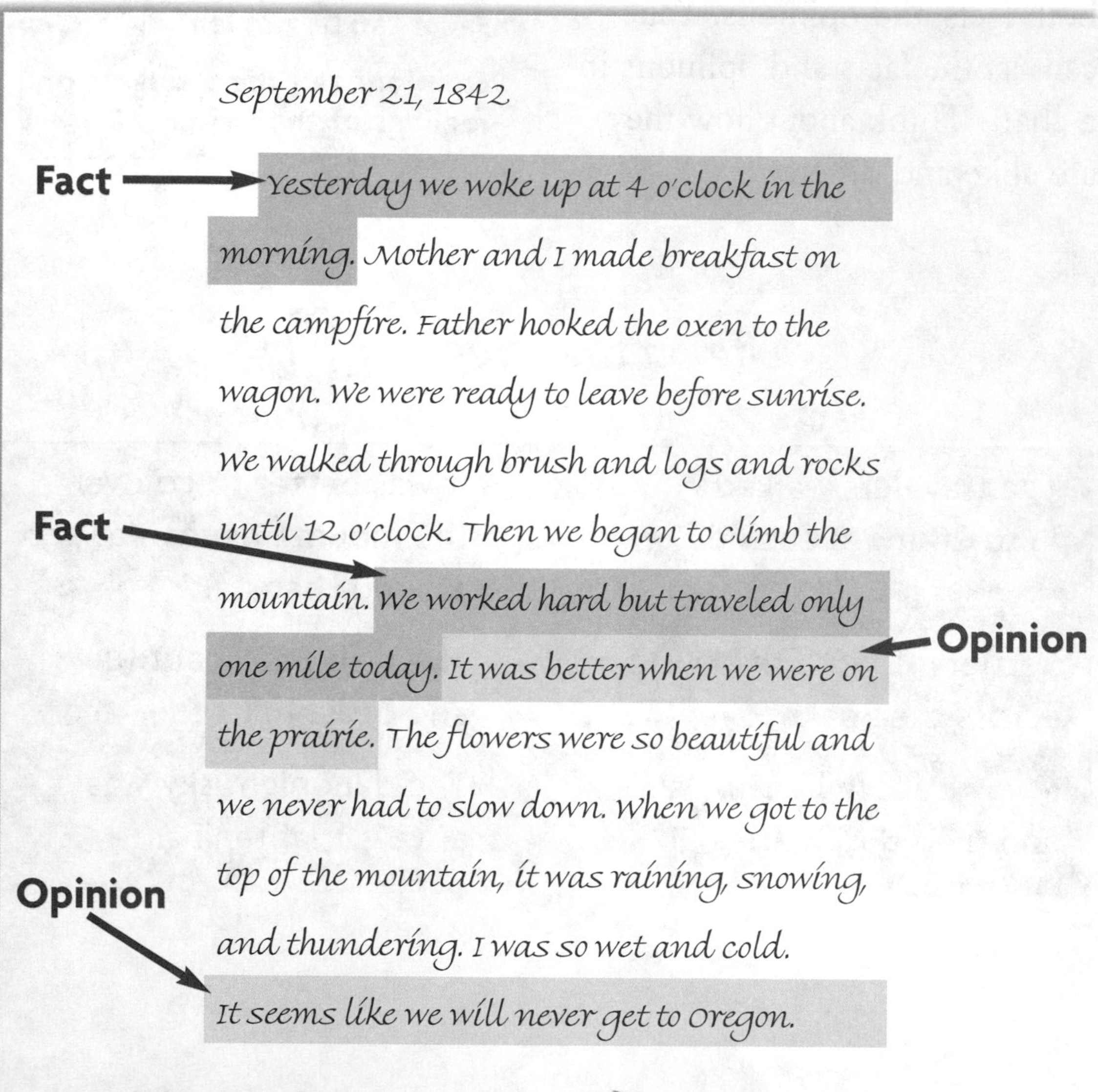

USE THIS SKILL

Tell Fact from Opinion

Read the paragraph below and find one fact and one opinion.

A Hard Journey

Traveling on the Oregon Trail was not easy. It could take six months to travel from Missouri to Oregon. The wagons were full of food and supplies, so many settlers had to walk the 2,000 miles. The worst part of the journey was the disease. In some wagon trains, nearly all of the settlers died because of sickness. Today, we should be happy that we don't have to travel on the Oregon Trail.

TEST TIP	Some tests ask you to find facts and opinions. Look for a statement that can be checked to find a fact. Look for a statement that tells someone's thoughts and feelings to find an opinion.

Skill 15

HOW TO

Draw Conclusions

Work in the Factory

Can you imagine working in a factory instead of going to school? In the 1800s, people of many ages worked in American factories.

A **factory** is a building or set of buildings in which things are made. The cotton mill in this picture is a factory in which yarn is made from raw cotton.

When you look at the picture of the cotton mill you look for information that helps you understand what you are seeing. When you draw a conclusion, you use information to decide what a picture or story means. A **conclusion** is a statement that sums up the meaning of information in a picture or story.

Cotton mill

By looking for information in the letter on this page, you can make conclusions. You can say that Anna liked the farm, but had to work to make money. You can say that both Elizabeth and Anna used to spin yarn by hand. You can also say that Anna wanted Elizabeth to write to her. These are conclusions that you can make based on the details in Anna's letter.

February 11, 1883

Dear Elizabeth,

I am writing to tell you that I have moved. I had to leave the farm and move into town. A factory has opened and I am working there. The factory is a cotton mill. At the mill, large machines spin the cotton by twisting it into yarn.

The factory makes the yarn so fast! It is also cheaper to buy than the yarn we used to spin by hand. Things from the factory are less expensive but working at the factory is hard. We work long hours and do not get much money. I miss the farm but each dollar I make helps the family. Please write when you can.

Your cousin,

Anna Harper

STEPS IN **Drawing Conclusions**

Use these steps to draw conclusions about the information on page 77.

1 Find Details

Look for the details that help you tell what the writing or picture means.

Details:
- The mill workers are young children.
- The children are standing on the machine.
- The children are not wearing shoes.

2 Use What You Know

What do you already know about what you are reading or seeing? Use what you know to understand the details you found.

What you know:
- Children don't work in factories in the U.S. today.
- Standing on machines and not wearing shoes is not safe.

3 Tell What It Means

Think about the details and what you already know to draw a conclusion. Make a statement that sums up the meaning of the information.

Conclusion:
It wasn't very safe for children to work in factories.

Mill Workers

Some boys and girls were so small they had to climb up on the spinning frame to mend broken threads and to put back empty bobbins.

EXAMPLE OF **Drawing Conclusions**

Read the passage below. It was written by Harriet Robinson. She worked in a mill and wrote about her life.

The early mill-girls were of different ages. Some were not over ten years old. A few were in middle life, but [most] were between the ages of sixteen and twenty five . . . The working hours of all the girls [was] from five o'clock in the morning until seven in the evening, with one half-hour each, for breakfast and dinner. Even the [very young girls] were forced to be on duty nearly fourteen hours a day.

Details

The girls at the mill were different ages.

Mill girls worked all day.

What I Know

Today boys and girls go to school during the day.

Conclusion

Mill girls could not go to school.

USE THIS SKILL

Draw Conclusions

Look at the picture below and draw a conclusion.

Mill workers often did the same job for many years.

Which is the best conclusion for the above photo?

A. Mill workers usually did many types of exciting jobs.

B. Only women worked in mills.

C. Mill workers had to wear hats and gloves for safety.

D. Most mill workers did the same job over and over.

TEST TIP

On a test, you may be asked to draw a conclusion. Read the question. Then skim the reading for details that will help you decide which answer is a correct conclusion.

Skill 16

HOW TO

Make a Decision

Earth-friendly Choices

"Use it up, wear it out, make it do, or do without!" This saying once described how people used Earth's resources. Today, we say, "Reduce, Reuse, Recycle!"

Recycling sign

Reduce means to use less of something. Using less packaging can mean less cardboard in landfills. **Reuse** means to find new uses for something. You could reuse an old bottle as a bank for coins. **Recycle** means to help turn waste material back into useful products. For example, used paper can be recycled to make new, clean paper.

Many people decide to reduce, reuse, and recycle. A **decision** is a choice you make. You make many decisions every day. Some decisions are simple, like deciding what to wear. Some decisions are difficult, like trying to decide if your school should reduce, reuse, and recycle certain materials.

STEPS IN Making a Decision

Follow these steps to make a decision.

1 Write the Question

Write down what you have to decide. Write it as a question, such as, "Should our school recycle paper?"

2 Name Your Choices

What choices do you have? List each choice. Each choice is a possible answer to your question.

3 Gather Information

Gather information about each choice. Collect all the information you can.

4 List the Pros and Cons

Study all the information you have. Make a list of the pros and cons for the choices. Pros and cons are the good and bad things about each choice.

5 Make Your Decision

Think about the pros and cons. Pick the choice that you think is best.

Some students decide to recycle in their school.

EXAMPLE OF **Making a Decision**

Hannah brought a juice box to school each day. After lunch, she threw the empty juice box in the trash. Hannah started to think about how many boxes were ending up in the trash. She asked herself how she could reduce the number of boxes she threw away. Read about how she made her decision.

Question

How will I reduce the number of boxes I throw away?

List of choices **List pros and cons**

Gather information

Choices	Pros	Cons
1. Drink water	It is easier to drink water because I won't have to carry it to school each day.	Juice has vitamins. It tastes better than water.
2. Take juice in a plastic bottle	The bottle can hold more juice than a juice box.	The bottle would need to be washed every day. The bottle could leak.
3. Take juice in a can	Cans can be recycled. A can would be as easy to carry as a juice box.	Cans cost more than juice boxes. I would use as many cans as juice boxes.

Decision

Take juice in a plastic bottle. I can reduce the number of boxes I throw away by reusing a container.

USE THIS SKILL

Make a Decision

Read the information below and make a decision about whether or not to reuse paper at school.

Reusing Paper at School

Schools use a lot of paper. Most schools throw away used paper but paper can be reused. You can put a big "X" over the writing on the front of the paper and use the back. Reused paper is not as neat as new paper because one side already has writing on it. Throwing away paper is easier because you don't have to save old paper. However, throwing away paper fills landfills and can cause more trees to be cut down.

1. What is your question?
2. What choices do you have?
3. Where could you find more information?
4. What are the pros and cons of reusing paper?
5. What is your decision? Why?

TEST TIP **Some tests ask you to explain if a decision is right or wrong. You will score higher if you use facts in your answer and write clearly.**

Skill 17

HOW TO
Take Notes

Patriotic Holidays

Flags, fireworks, and parades — it must be the Fourth of July! On July 4 in 1776, the Declaration of Independence was signed. This document explained why the colonies wanted to be free from Britain.

The Fourth of July is a patriotic holiday. A **patriotic holiday** is a holiday that honors a part of your country's history.

Taking notes can help you remember information about patriotic holidays. When you **take notes,** you write down important information about a topic. Notes can help you organize facts. You can take notes when you write a report or prepare an oral report.

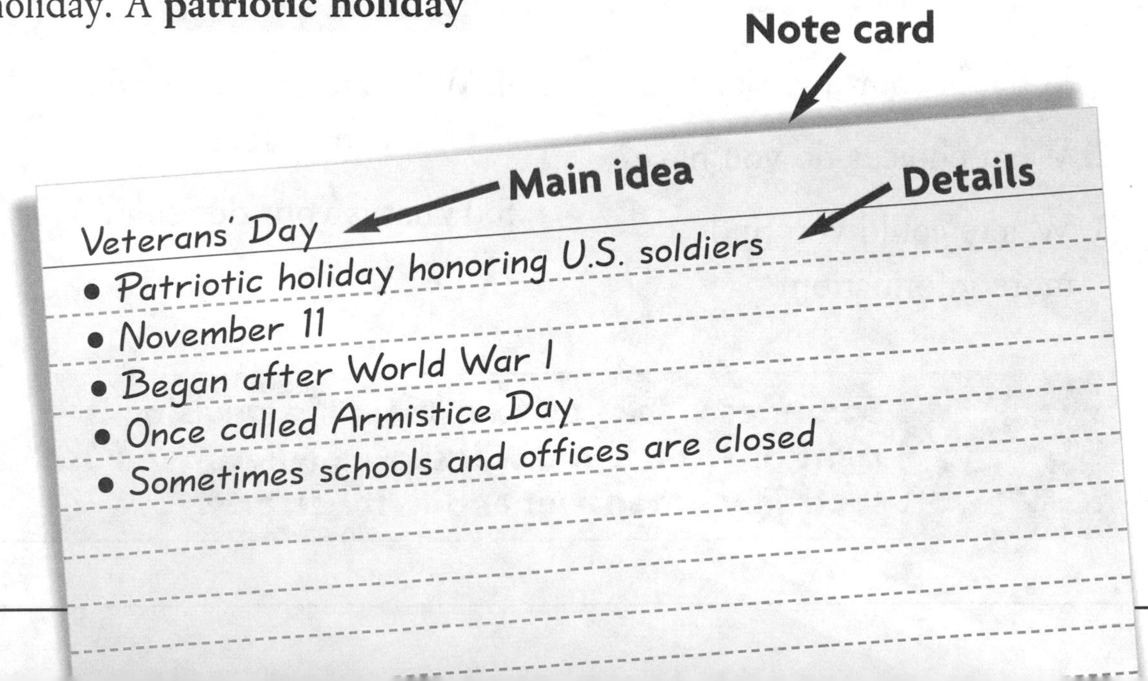

Note card

Main idea

Details

Veterans' Day
- Patriotic holiday honoring U.S. soldiers
- November 11
- Began after World War I
- Once called Armistice Day
- Sometimes schools and offices are closed

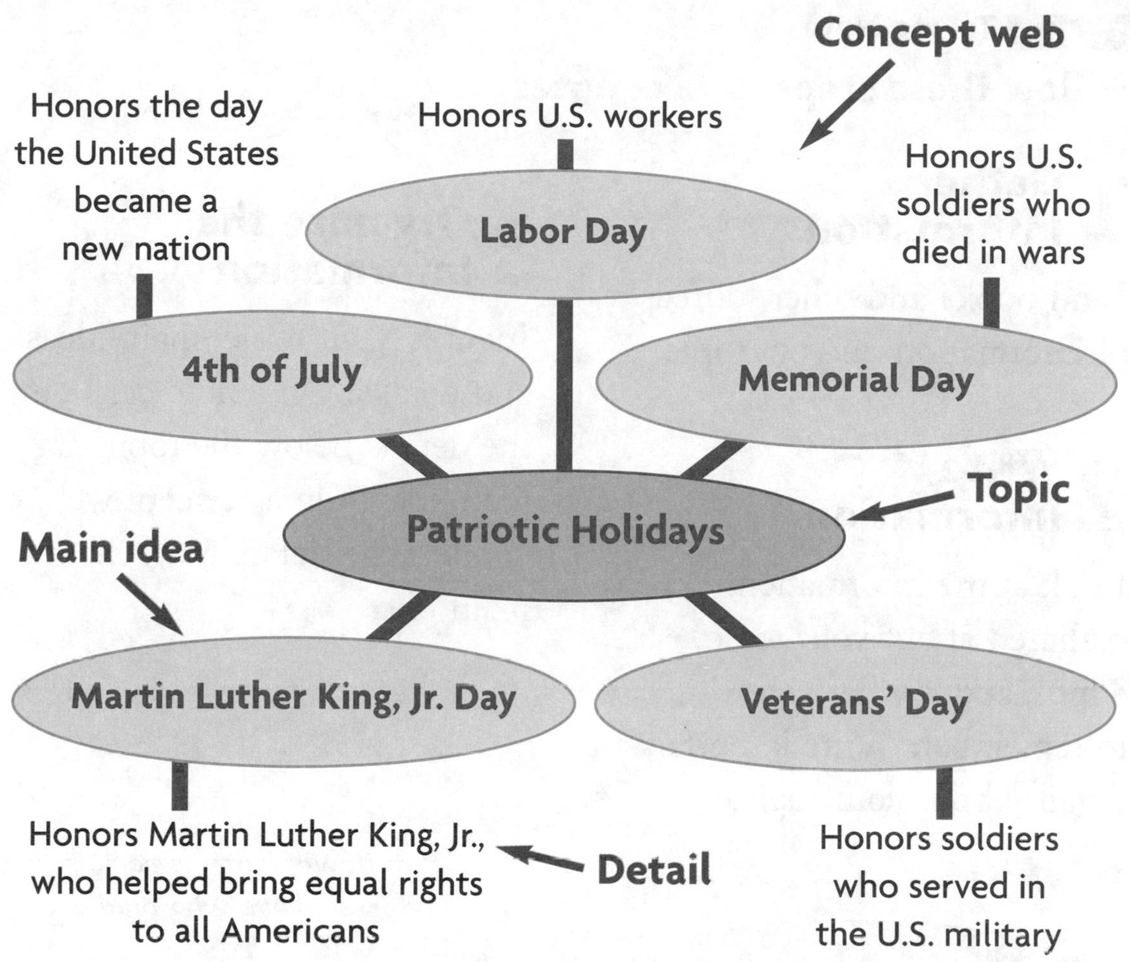

Putting information in a concept web is one way of taking notes. On a concept web, you put the topic in the middle. Then you connect main ideas to the topic. You can then connect details, like important facts, that explain each main idea.

Note cards can also be used to take notes. On a note card, you can put the topic or main idea at the top. Then you can put details, like important facts, below. Both note cards and concept webs can help you organize information.

STEPS IN **Taking Notes**

Follow these steps to take notes.

1 Gather Information

Find books and other sources of information on your topic.

2 Write Information

Look at the information you gathered about your topic. Think about what you want to remember. Write important details about your topic.

3 Organize the Information

Identify your topic, main ideas, and details. On a note card put the details below the topic or main idea. On a concept web, connect the details to each main idea.

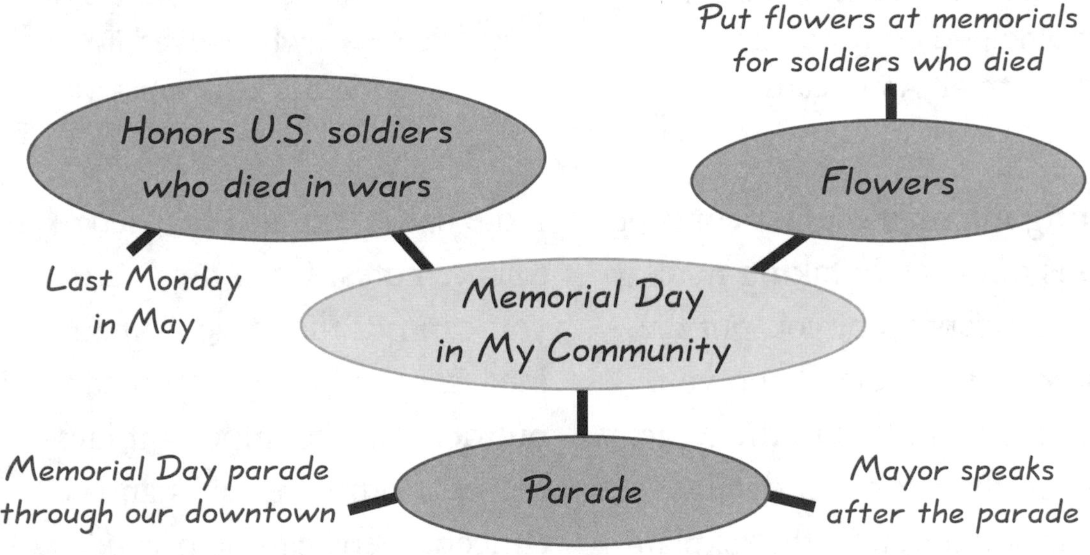

4 Review Your Notes

TIP Notes don't have to be in complete sentences. They should be short.

After you take notes, look through them. Do they help you remember important facts about your topic? Add anything else that you think is important to include in your notes.

Memorial Day

- Started after Civil War to honor soldiers
- Holiday first called Decoration Day
- Included soldiers who died in all wars after World War I
- Name of holiday changed to Memorial Day after World War I
- Grandfather—celebrates Memorial Day in Washington, D.C.

Review and add any other notes

My grandfather in Washington, D.C., last summer

EXAMPLE OF Taking Notes

Look at the note card below to see how you can take notes from an encyclopedia article for a report.

Labor Day

LABOR DAY

Labor Day is a holiday that is celebrated in the United States and other countries. It is a national holiday in the United States. The first celebration of Labor Day in the United States was in New York City in 1882. There was a parade and many speeches. Congress made it an official holiday in 1894. Labor Day is celebrated on the first Monday in September every year in the United States and Canada. In many other countries, Labor Day is on the first of May.

See also: LABOR UNIONS; NATIONAL HOLIDAYS; PATRIOTIC HOLIDAYS

Gather information

Organize the information

Main idea

Labor Day

- First celebration in New York City in 1882
- Parade and speeches
- Made an official holiday in 1894
- First Monday in September in U.S. and Canada
- Started by Central Labor Union as a holiday in honor of workers

Details

Review and add any other notes

USE THIS SKILL

Take Notes

Read about Presidents' Day below. Then take notes on note cards or on a concept web.

Presidents' Day

Presidents' Day is a day honoring past presidents of the United States. While the Revolutionary War was still being fought, people celebrated George Washington's birthday on February 22. The tradition lasted more than a hundred years. In 1866, people began celebrating Abraham Lincoln's birthday, too. His birthday was February 12.

Both days became patriotic holidays. Schools were closed. Government offices also closed. People made patriotic speeches about the two great presidents.

In 1968, Congress moved the celebration of Washington's birthday to the third Monday in February. In 1971, President Richard Nixon ordered that the day become Presidents' Day —a day to honor all U.S. presidents.

TEST TIP

You may be asked to write an essay on a test. Before you write, take notes. This can help you remember important points as you write your essay.

Skill 18

HOW TO

Recognize a Point of View

Chief Joseph

Since the explorers Lewis and Clark went through the Northwest in 1805, the Native American tribe called the Nez Perce had peace with white settlers. Many years later this peace was lost and the Nez Perce leader, Chief Joseph, was forced to lead his people away from their homeland.

During his life, Joseph had many experiences with people who were not Native Americans. Because of his different experiences, Chief Joseph's feelings about the settlers changed throughout his life.

A person's **point of view** is the way that a person looks at something based on his or her ideas, feelings, and experiences. Look for Chief Joseph's point of view in this reading.

The first white men who came to our country were named Lewis and Clark . . . They talked straight and our people gave them a great feast as proof that their hearts were friendly . . . All the Nez Perce made friends with Lewis and Clark and agreed to let them pass through their country and never to make war on white men.

–Chief Joseph

STEPS IN Recognizing a Point of View

Use these steps to recognize point of view.

1 Identify the Speaker

Find out who wrote or spoke the words that you are reading.

2 Find the Topic

Find out what the speaker is talking about. What is the main idea of the speaker's speech or story?

3 Find Events and Feelings

Identify the events that took place. What actually happened? Then look for words that tell how the speaker thinks and feels about those events.

4 Find the Point of View

Explain how the person thinks and feels about the topic based on his or her ideas, feelings, and experiences.

Speaker: Chief Joseph
Topic: The peace between the Nez Perce and white men
Events/Feelings:
Events–Nez Perce gave Lewis and Clark a feast.
Feelings–Their hearts were friendly and they agreed to let them pass through their country.
Point of View:
Based on meeting Lewis and Clark, Chief Joseph liked white men and never wanted war.

EXAMPLE OF **Recognizing a Point of View**

As you read this speech, think about who is talking and what he thinks and feels.

Speaker → **Chief Joseph's Speech about the Mistreatment of the Nez Perce** ← **Topic**

Events →

For a short time we lived quietly. But this could not last. White men . . . stole a great many horses from us and we could not get them back because we were Indians . . . They drove off a great many of our cattle. Some white men branded our young cattle so they could claim them. We had no friends who would plead our cause before the law councils. . . . We gave up some of our country to the white men, thinking that then we could have peace. We were mistaken. The white men would not let us alone.

Chief Joseph

USE THIS SKILL

Recognize a Point of View

Read the passage and answer the questions below.

Surrender Speech of Chief Joseph, 1877

I am tired of fighting. Our chiefs are killed . . . The old men are all dead . . . He who led the young men are dead. It is cold, and we have no blankets. The little children are freezing to death. My people, some of them, have run away to the hills, and have no blankets, no food . . . I want to have time to look for my children, and see how many of them I can find. Maybe I shall find them among the dead. Hear me, my chiefs. I am tired. My heart is sick and sad. From where the sun now stands I will fight no more forever.

1. Who is the speaker and what is he talking about?
2. How does he feel?
3. What is his point of view about war? Do you think he will fight in the future? Why?

TEST TIP **When you are looking for a person's point of view on a test, look for words that tell how the person feels.**

Skill 19

HOW TO

Understand an Advertisement

What Do You Buy?

If you got money for your birthday to buy a toy, how would you decide which kind of toy to buy? Many companies use advertisements to get you to buy their toys or other products.

An **advertisement,** or ad, is something that tells about a product or service. Ads are in magazines, on television, in newspapers, and many other places. They can help you decide if you want to buy a product.

Look at the two cereal ads on the next page. Based on the information in the ads, which cereal would you buy? You can use the following steps to help you understand advertisements and decide which product to buy.

1 Look for Facts

Find the facts in each ad. The prices and the sizes of products are important facts that are often in ads. Both of the cereal ads tell you the price of the cereal. The ads also tell that Energy Puffs has vitamins in it and Choco Crisps has a toy.

2 Look for Loaded Words

Loaded words are words that try to make you buy the product. The loaded words in the cereal ads are *new, more, best, only,* and *better*. They are not facts but words that try to make you buy the product.

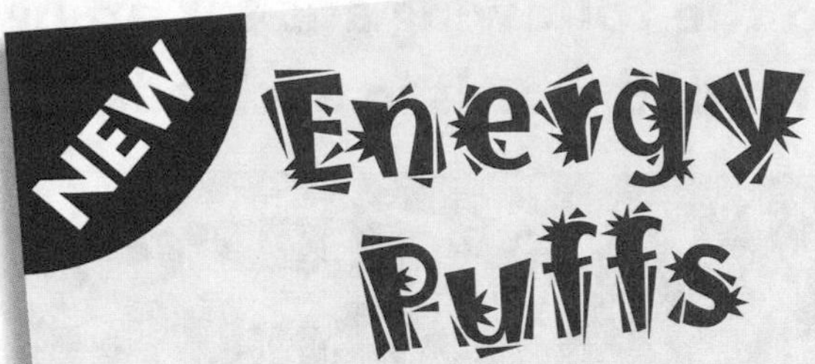

★ Packed with vitamins for more energy every day.
★ The best in flavor and nutrients is **Energy Puffs** for only $4.20!

Choco Crisps

Taste **better** than ever and a **TOY** in every box!

New and **improved** flavor for only $3.80!

3 Compare the Facts

Compare all of the facts. Which facts are most important to you? If vitamins are more important to you than a free toy, you would probably buy the Energy Puffs. If the price is more important to you, then you might buy the Choco Crisps.

EXAMPLE OF Understanding an Advertisement

Read the following ads for orange juice. Find the facts and the loaded words in each advertisement.

Healthy Kids OJ

Builds more powerful bodies and tastes great!

A 16-ounce bottle and a coupon for a FREE orange, all for just $2

Loaded words

Fact

Fact

Compare the facts

Product	Size	Price	Extras
Nature's Best	32-ounce carton	$3	Added calcium
Healthy Kids	16-ounce bottle	$2	Free orange

USE THIS SKILL

Understand an Advertisement

Read the ads below and answer the following questions.

1. What facts can you find in each ad?
2. What loaded words are in each ad?
3. By comparing the facts in the ads, which product would you buy? Why?

TEST TIP **You may be asked about an advertisement on a test. Look carefully at the words in the ad. Be sure you understand the difference between facts and loaded words.**

Skill 20

HOW TO

Work in a Group

Planning a Business

Think about your favorite food. Who makes it? How is it made? Many of the foods and things you buy are made by people who work together in a group to make a product.

Working in a group is when two or more people help each other achieve a goal. At home, you may work with your family to make meals or clean. In sports, you may work with your teammates to play a game and score points. In school, you may work together with your classmates on a group project.

You and some of your classmates may want to work together to have a lemonade stand to raise money for a class picnic. Before you start, your group may want to make a business plan. A **business plan** is a plan that tells what people starting a business are going to do and how they will do it. A business plan could help your group get ready to make and sell your lemonade.

TIP Listen carefully to each member of your group. Respect each person's thoughts and feelings.

STEPS IN Working in a Group

Here are steps to help you work together in a group.

1 Decide on Your Goal

Decide on the goal of the project. Each person should have a chance to share his or her ideas. Make a list of everyone's ideas and choose the idea, or a combination of different people's ideas, that the group agrees is best. Write down your goal.

2 Figure Out Tasks

When you have agreed on your goal, your group should decide what needs to be done to achieve the goal. What materials will you need to buy? What needs to be made? In what order does each thing need to be done? Figure out the tasks that need to be done to achieve your goal.

3 Choose Jobs

Each person in the group should choose which jobs he or she will do. Make sure all of the tasks have been taken. The work should be divided as evenly as possible.

4 Write a Schedule

When does each task need to be done? Group members should agree when they will have each task finished.

Group Plan

A. Our goal is: ____________

B. Things we need to do:

1. ____________
2. ____________

C. Jobs for each group member:

Name__________ Job__________

Name__________ Job__________

EXAMPLE OF **Working in a Group**

Think about how the students worked together to make the following Group Plan for a class project.

Group goal

Business Plan for Lemonade Stand

A. Our project goal is to do a business plan for a lemonade stand

Tasks to be done

B. Things we need to do:

1. Describe our business—tell who we are and what we will sell
2. Tell about our market—name the people we hope will buy our lemonade and why
3. Tell how we will make our product—tell what materials we will need and how we will make our lemonade
4. Tell how we will advertise—how we will let people know about our lemonade stand and get them to come
5. Tell how much money we hope to make—tell how much our materials will cost and what our price for lemonade will be

Jobs for each person

C. Jobs for each group member:

Name: LaShawna Job: Tell about our business and market
Name: Sarah Job: Tell how we will make the lemonade
Name: Robert Job: Tell how we will advertise
Name: José Job: Tell how much lemonade we need to sell

Schedule

D. Schedule:

Job: Our business and market Date due: April 6
Job: How we will make our product Date due: April 8
Job: How we will advertise Date due: April 8
Job: How much money we will make Date due: April 9

Final Project due date: **April 11**

USE THIS SKILL

Work in a Group

Imagine that your school is having a fair. Work in a group to make a plan to sell popcorn at the school fair. The information below can help you get started.

Business Plan for Popcorn Sale

A. Our goal is: make a plan to sell popcorn at the school fair

B. Things we need to do:

1. ____________________
2. ____________________
3. ____________________

C. Jobs for each group member:

Name ____________ Job ____________

Name ____________ Job ____________

Name ____________ Job ____________

D. Schedule:

Job ____________ Date due ____________

Job ____________ Date due ____________

TEST TIP

For all tests you need to plan your time. First find out how many questions are on the test. Skip any questions that are too hard and go back to them if you have time.

Writing and Research Skills

Skill 21

HOW TO

Write a Paragraph

Lessons from Lincoln

When you think of Abraham Lincoln, what do you think about? You might think of the sixteenth president. You might think of a man who helped to end slavery. You might think of a tall man with a dark beard.

One thing you might not think of is a man who was very skillful at putting ideas together. Lincoln was a great speaker and writer. He knew how to organize his thoughts and put them into paragraphs that were easy to understand.

Abraham Lincoln

A **paragraph** is a group of two or more sentences about one subject. A paragraph has a topic sentence, a body, and a closing sentence. Each of these parts tells about the subject of the paragraph.

STEPS IN **Writing a Paragraph**

Use these steps to write a paragraph.

1 Pick Your Subject

Plan what your paragraph will be about. A paragraph should have only one main idea.

2 Write a Topic Sentence

A topic sentence introduces the subject and tells the main idea of the paragraph. It is usually at the beginning of the paragraph.

3 Write the Body

The body of the paragraph is made of sentences that tell about the subject. Use details to describe or explain your subject. Put the sentences in the order in which they happened.

4 Write a Closing

The closing is the last sentence of the paragraph. It should wrap up the paragraph by reminding the reader about the subject of the paragraph.

Paragraph

Topic Sentence

- Introduces subject
- Tells the main idea of the paragraph
- Begins paragraph

Body

- Sentences that tell about the subject
- Uses details to describe or explain subject

Closing

- Reminds the reader about the subject
- Ends paragraph

EXAMPLE OF Writing a Paragraph

Read the passage below about Abraham Lincoln and think about each part of the paragraph.

A Love of Learning

Topic sentence

Abraham Lincoln was a man who loved learning. His parents could not read or write, so Lincoln taught himself. He went to school only one year, but he borrowed books from neighbors whenever he could. Lincoln was interested in law, so he bought and borrowed law books to study. In 1836, he passed the Illinois Bar Exam and became a lawyer. Lincoln's education helped him in many jobs. During his life, Lincoln was a postmaster, farmer, storekeeper, surveyor, lawyer, legislator, and the President of the United States. The education that Lincoln gave himself helped him go far in life.

Body

Closing

Abraham Lincoln, 1809–1865

USE THIS SKILL

Write a Paragraph

Write a good paragraph using the sentences below.

- When Lincoln became President in 1860, he and his family moved into the White House in Washington, D.C.
- Long after his death, we still remember Lincoln as a man who traveled from the farm to the White House to become one of our nation's greatest leaders.
- In 1834, he became a member of the Illinois State Legislature.
- Abraham Lincoln was born on February 12, 1809, in Hodgenville, Kentucky.
- Abraham Lincoln lived in different places in the United States.
- Lincoln left farm life and moved to New Salem, Illinois, in 1831.

TEST TIP

Some tests ask you to identify the main idea of a reading passage. The correct answer will be the one that best summarizes what the reading passage is mostly about.

Skill 22

HOW TO

Write an Explanation

The Colonial Kitchen

In colonial times, cooks didn't have microwave ovens or blenders. They didn't even have electricity in their homes. Food was cooked over an open fire.

When you cook, you might use a recipe. A recipe is a step-by-step explanation of how to make a certain kind of food. An **explanation** tells how something is done. Recipes give the details about the ingredients you need and how to use them.

A colonial kitchen

STEPS IN **Writing an Explanation**

Use these steps to write an explanation that tells how to do something.

Kettle Beans

1 cup beans
3 cups water
1/4 cup molasses
1 large piece of salt pork

Put all of the ingredients together in a kettle.
Mix everything together.
Put pot over fire and cook overnight.

1 Identify Your Topic

Tell what it is that you are doing or making.

TIP **It sometimes helps to act out what you are explaining. Acting out a process will help you remember all the steps.**

2 Make a List

Make a list or tell everything that is needed to make or do the project.

3 Explain the Steps

Explain each step of the process in order. Give all of the details needed to do each step correctly.

EXAMPLE OF **Writing an Explanation**

Read the explanation below of how to make green corn pudding. Green corn is fresh corn used to make this popular colonial food.

Topic → Green Corn Pudding

Ingredients ← **List of ingredients or materials**

4-5 ears of green corn
3 egg yolks
2 tablespoons butter
2 tablespoons brown sugar
1 teaspoon fine sea salt
2 cups milk
3 egg whites

Steps

1. Preheat oven to 350°.
2. Use a knife to cut corn kernels from the cob. You should get about 2 cups of corn.
3. Scrape the cob to get all the juices.
4. Beat egg yolks until they are thick.
5. Mix together the egg yolks, corn, butter, sugar, and salt.
6. Slowly blend in milk.
7. Fold in beaten egg whites.
8. Gently put the mixture into a buttered baking dish and bake 45-50 minutes.

USE THIS SKILL

Write an Explanation

Write an explanation of how to make the food shown below. It was popular in the colonial times and is still popular today. If you have never made this food, write an explanation of how to buy this food at a movie theater.

Popcorn

TEST TIP	On a test, you may have to put the steps of a process in the right order. Look for words like **first, then, next,** and **last** to help you put the steps in order.

Skill 23

HOW TO

Write a Comparison

Colonial Schools

Look around your classroom. What do you see? Desks? Textbooks? Computers? How do you think your classroom might compare to a classroom in the 1600s and 1700s?

A good way to learn about people, places, and things is to compare them to something you know. When you make a **comparison,** you tell how two or more things are alike.

Read the following passage. Can you tell how colonial and current textbooks compare?

Hornbook

In classrooms today, you'll find textbooks with many pages and pictures. Colonial schoolrooms had a kind of textbook called a hornbook. A hornbook was a paddle-shaped board with a sheet of paper on it. The paper usually had the alphabet, numerals, and prayers written on it.

STEPS IN Writing a Comparison

Use these steps to write a comparison.

1 Pick the Topics

Choose two topics you want to compare.

2 List Features

Write down features, or details, about each of the topics you are comparing. Then find the features that both topics have in common.

3 Write About the Common Features

Before writing your comparison, you can make a Venn diagram like the one below to help you find common features. Begin your comparison with a topic sentence that tells what two topics you are comparing. Then use your list of common features to make sentences that tell how the two topics are alike.

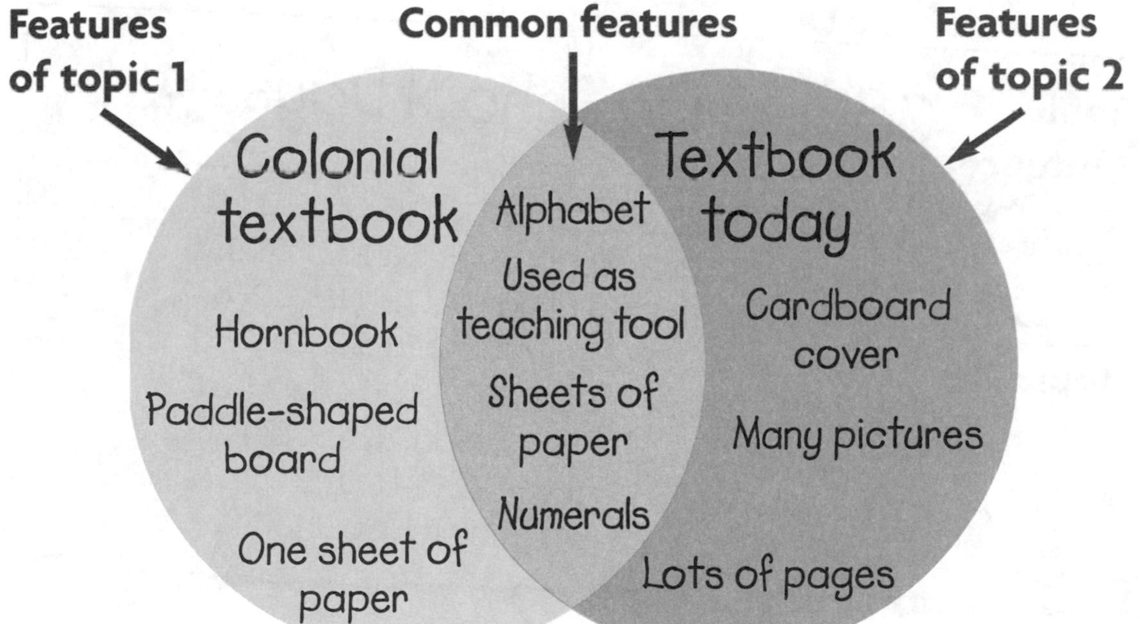

EXAMPLE OF Writing a Comparison

As you read the story below, think about how a colonial classroom is like your own.

School in Colonial America

A school day in colonial times started in the morning. Most students spent the day studying reading, writing, simple math, and prayers. Some wealthier schools also taught foreign languages, higher math, science, and social manners. Students used hornbooks to learn the alphabet, numbers, and prayers. They recited most lessons. Most colonial schools had only one room for students of all ages to share. Many schools were for either boys or girls. Only a few let boys and girls go to class together.

Comparing School Days

Topic sentence

Topic 1

Topic 2

Some things about my school day and a colonial school day are the same. Both school days start in the morning. Reading, writing, math, and science are studied in both schools. Numbers and the alphabet are learned by students in both schools. Each school also has books that the students use to study their lessons.

Common features

USE THIS SKILL

Write a Comparison

Write a comparison of the two classrooms shown in the two pictures below.

Colonial classroom

A classroom today

TEST TIP	
When you are asked to make comparisons on a test, think about how things are similar. Be sure to check each answer against the information in the reading passage.	

Skill 24

HOW TO

Write a Journal Entry

An American Thanksgiving

In 1621, the Pilgrim Governor William Bradford called for a day of thanksgiving. The Pilgrims and Native Americans celebrated their crops, their homes, and their friendship.

What would it have been like to be at that celebration? What would you have thought and felt? A **journal** is a kind of notebook in which you can write your thoughts, feelings, and memories.

An early American Thanksgiving

In a journal entry, you can tell about the interesting things you have seen, heard, and done. You can also describe how things looked, felt, tasted, and smelled.

Journal entries often have many details that tell about your personal thoughts, activities, or ideas. Look for personal thoughts and feelings in the journal entry below.

October 14, 1621

It's getting cold and the leaves are turning red. I am happy that we had a good harvest. We will save most of our food for the winter. The rest we will share with Chief Massasoit and our other new friends.

I can't wait to see Squanto! Last spring, he showed us how to plant corn and get sap from maple trees. He also showed us which plants are poisonous and which ones are not. He is a Wampanoag Indian but he can speak English. It seems like he knows everything. I am happy he is our friend.

TIP **You can look in your journal to find ideas for stories and poems.**

STEPS IN Writing a Journal Entry

Use these steps to write a journal entry.

1 Get Your Tools

Gather a notebook and pen or pencil. Pick a spot that's quiet. Find a time when you can write each day.

2 Date Your Entry

Before you begin to write, put the month, day, and year on the page. The date will tell you when you wrote your entry if you read your journal later.

3 Write Your Entry

Write whatever comes to your mind. As you write, use details to describe your thoughts, feelings, or memories.

4 Make a Drawing

You can use drawings, diagrams, and lists in your journal. Pictures can help to show the things or events that you are describing in your journal entry.

5 Read and Reflect

Go back every week or two and read your journal entries. Your writing can remind you of things you might have forgotten. You can also learn a lot about yourself through your writing.

October 17, 1621

We have all been so busy that I've had little time to write. We worked in the fields picking squash and corn. The men hunted. We could sometimes hear the shots from their muskets. We cooked and baked for many days. Everyone in Plymouth has been busy.

Detail

Drawing

Mother and me picking corn

October 18, 1621

When everything was cooked and ready, we shared a wonderful meal! These were some of the foods at our celebration: broiled cod and bass, roasted goose, boiled turkey, corn pudding, roasted venison, hominy pudding, Holland cheese, boiled squashes, and dried whortleberries.

List of details

EXAMPLE OF **Writing a Journal Entry**

Read the journal entry below. Look at how the writer used details to describe his thoughts and feelings.

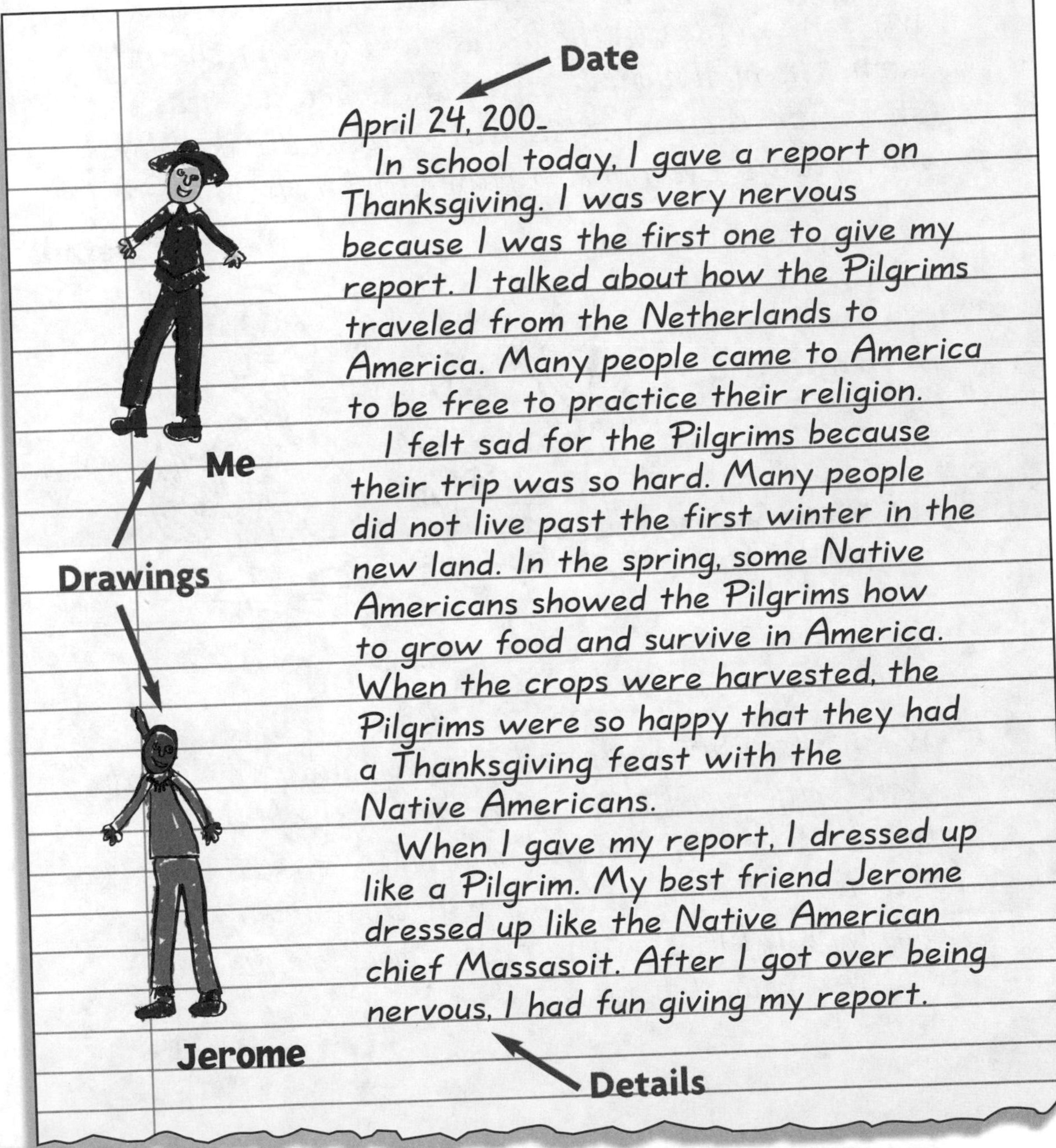

USE THIS SKILL

Write a Journal Entry

Look at the picture below. Pretend you are one of the people in the photo and write a journal entry about your day. Use details to describe the event, the food, and the people.

The summer block party on my street

TEST TIP

On a test, you may read a journal entry and answer questions about it. To answer the questions, look for details in the journal entry. The correct answer will contain information from the journal.

Skill 25

HOW TO

Do an Interview

Choosing Goods and Services

Do you have a pet? If you do, where do you go to get its food, to have its check-ups, or to get it groomed? You choose certain goods and services every time that you pay for something.

Goods are things people make, like pet food. **Services** are things people do, like giving your pet a check-up or grooming. You may choose a certain pet food because it is the least expensive. There may be other reasons why you buy certain goods or services.

To find out why people choose the goods and services they do, you could do an interview. An **interview** is a meeting in which one person asks questions and another person answers them. Doing an interview is one way to gather information.

Suppose you had to write a report about the goods and services people buy for their pets. For your report, you could interview pet owners in your community. You could ask them questions about the goods and services they buy. Follow the steps on the next page to do an interview.

STEPS IN **Doing an Interview**

1 List the People

Think about the topic of your report and what you want to find out in your interview. Then make a list of people who could give you information about your topic. Ask each person on your list if you can interview him or her and why you would like to do the interview. If the person agrees, plan a date and time for the interview.

2 List the Questions

Write out each of the questions you would like to ask during the interview. Put the questions in the order you want to ask them.

3 Hold the Interview

Take notes as you get answers to your questions. At the end of the interview, thank the person for sharing his or her time.

Interview Notes with Mr. Johnson

1. What pet food do you buy?
   - Tasty Feast Cat Food
2. Do you buy any other goods, like treats or toys, for your pet?
   - Catnip ball
   - Feather toy
3. Are there any services you pay to have done, like grooming or going to the vet?
   - Goes to the vet once a year

EXAMPLE OF Doing an Interview

Read the notebook page below. It shows the questions that a student asked and the notes that were taken during the interview.

Tuesday at 4:00 P.M.

Interview with Ms. Lastilla about Goods and Services

1. *What kind of pet do you have?*
   A dog named Prince
2. *What kind of pet food do you buy?*
   Bow Wow Dog Food
3. *Why do you buy this pet food?*
   Because it's the pet store's brand of dog food and the vet recommended it
4. *Are there other goods, like treats or toys, that you buy for your pet?*
   Dog biscuits and chew bones
5. *Do you pay to have any services done for your pet, like taking it to the vet?*
   Yes—she takes Prince to the vet and also has his hair cut and nails clipped every two months

USE THIS SKILL

Do an Interview

Interview at least two people who have pets. Find out what goods and services they buy for their pets.

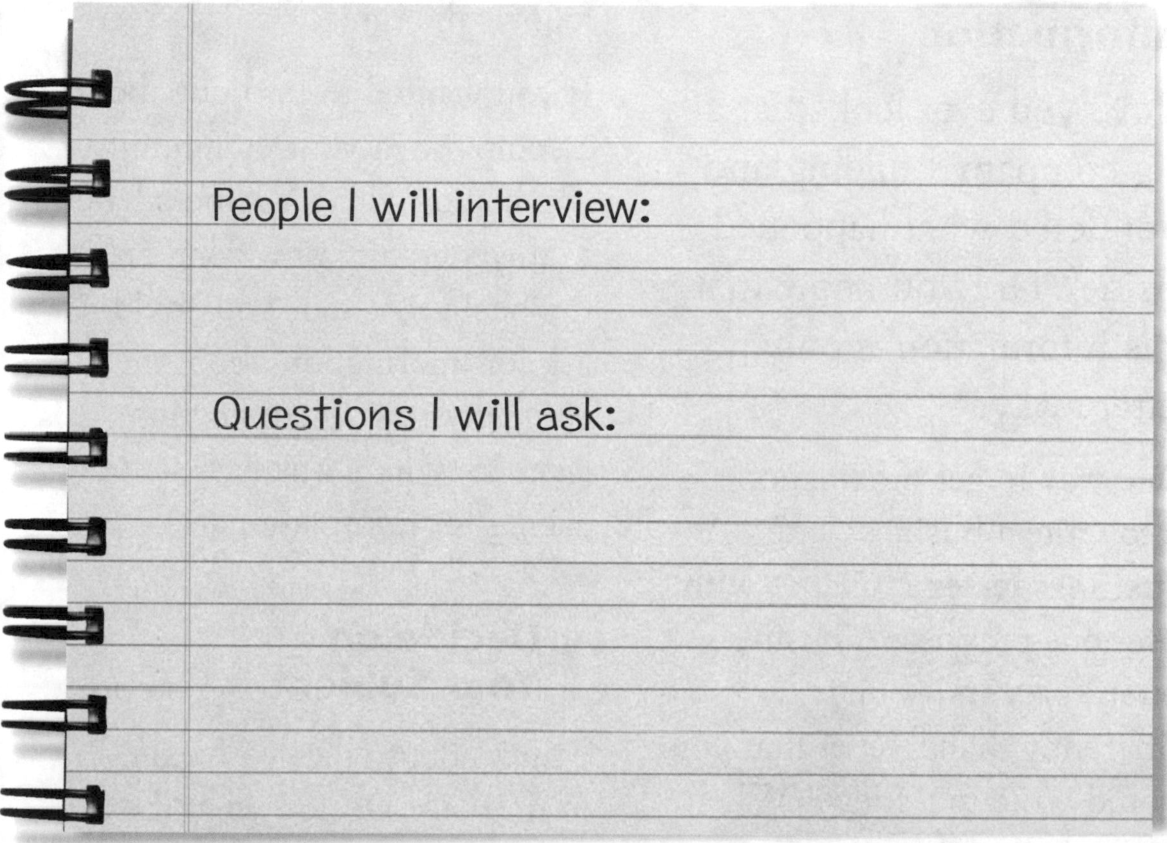

TEST TIP

Some tests may ask you to read a passage and tell how someone feels about a topic. First identify the topic. Then look for action words, such as cry, dance, or laugh, that could tell how the person feels about the topic.

Skill 26

HOW TO

Write a Business Letter

Getting the Inside Information

Have you ever looked at a big company building and wondered what happened inside? Did you know that this information is only a letter away?

One way to get information is to write a business letter. A **business letter** is a letter with a serious purpose. A business letter looks and sounds differently than a letter that you would write to a friend. When you write to a friend, you probably write about many subjects, such as things you have recently seen and done. A business letter is more serious than a letter to a friend. It is about one subject and always follows the same form.

If you wanted to find out about a company in your community, you could write a business letter to the company president. In the business letter, you could ask for information about the company. Use the following steps to write a business letter asking for information.

1 Decide on Your Subject

Think about what you want to find out. Decide what the subject or topic of your business letter will be. Then think about what questions you want answered. List your questions and make them as clear and specific as you can.

STEPS IN Writing a Business Letter

2 Follow the Form

Your business letter should have six parts: a heading, inside address, salutation, body, closing, and signature.

Parts of a Business Letter

Heading—your address and the date

Inside address—who you are writing and his or her address

Salutation—greeting the person, using Ms. for women and Mr. for men

Body—the main part of the letter

Closing—the end of the letter

Signature—your name, signed and typed

Not a specific question

Questions I Could Ask

~~Tell me everything you can about your company.~~

What does your company do?

How many people work there?

Clear questions

3 Draft Your Letter

Begin your letter by telling why you are writing and what information you need. Then ask any questions you have. End by thanking the person for his or her help.

4 Check Your Work

Proofread for spelling, grammar, capitalization, and punctuation. Then have a teacher or family member read over your work.

5 Send Your Letter

Make a neat copy to send.

EXAMPLE OF Writing a Business Letter

Read the business letter below. Look at each part of the letter and the form that it follows.

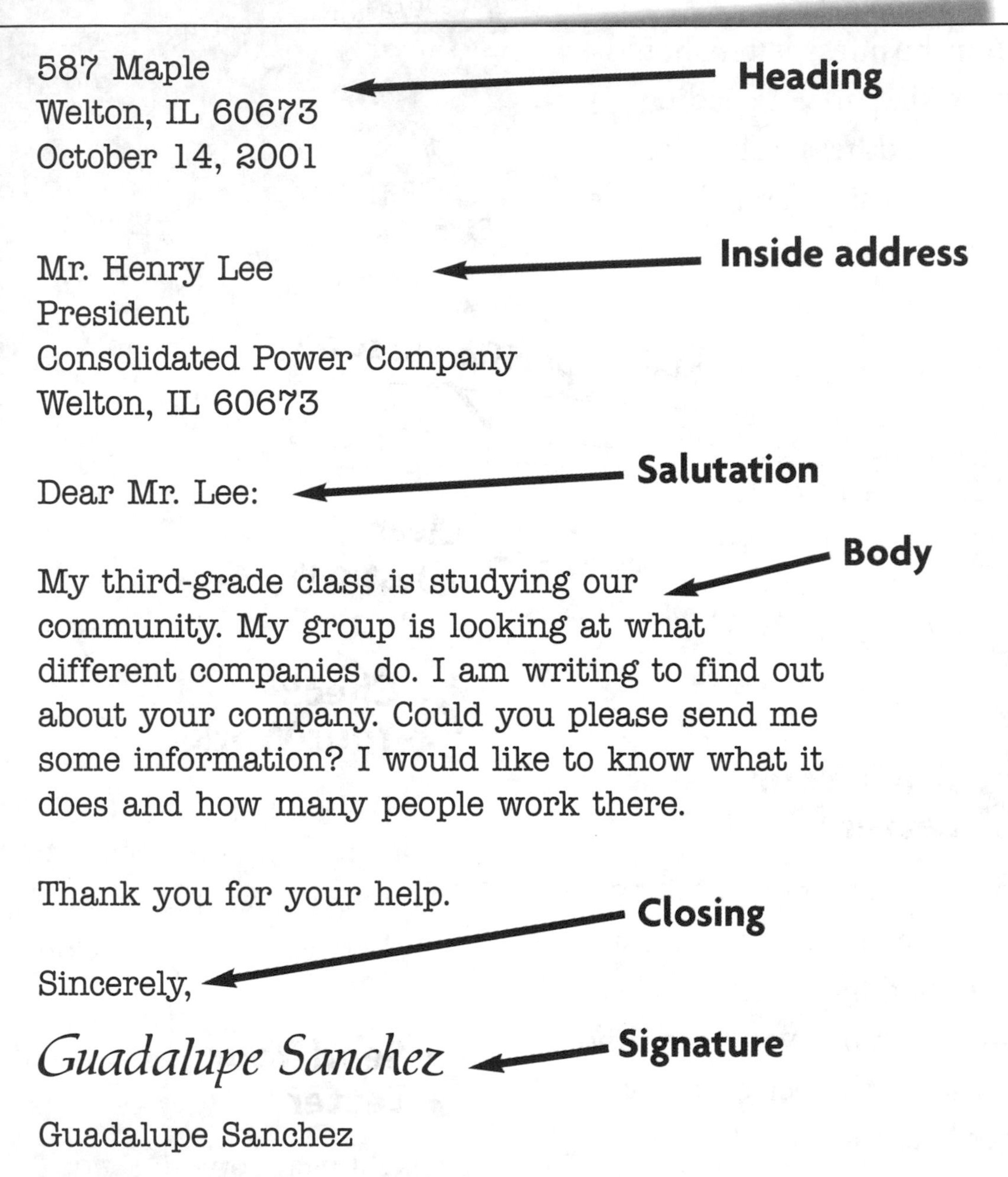

587 Maple
Welton, IL 60673
October 14, 2001

Mr. Henry Lee
President
Consolidated Power Company
Welton, IL 60673

Dear Mr. Lee:

My third-grade class is studying our community. My group is looking at what different companies do. I am writing to find out about your company. Could you please send me some information? I would like to know what it does and how many people work there.

Thank you for your help.

Sincerely,

Guadalupe Sanchez

Guadalupe Sanchez

USE THIS SKILL

Write a Business Letter

Write a business letter to the following person. Ask for information about what her company makes. Use the form below to help you get started.

____

____

____

Ms. Mary Connor
President
Global Software
190 Hemingway Parkway
Mountain View, CA 94040

Dear ____________________:

TEST TIP

Some tests may ask you to punctuate a letter. Be sure to use a comma to separate a city from a state, the day's date from the year, and again after the closing.

Skill 27

HOW TO

Write a Skit

The Boston Tea Party

When you hear *tea party,* you might think of teapots and china dishes. In 1773, a different kind of tea party took place. It was the Boston Tea Party.

In the middle of the night on December 16, 1773, a group of American colonists dressed up as Native Americans and sneaked onto a guarded British ship. They dumped 342 chests of tea into the Boston harbor because they were angry about British taxes. The taxes were extra amounts of money that the colonists had to pay to Britain when they bought certain things.

The Boston Tea Party

In May of 1773, the British Parliament passed the Tea Act. It made colonists pay taxes on tea. It also made special rules for a British tea company called the East India Company. These rules helped the British company and hurt American tea companies. Many colonists didn't think this was right. Instead of buying the British tea, colonists threw it into the harbor to show they thought the rules were unfair.

If you wanted to tell the story of the Boston Tea Party, you could write a skit. A **skit** is a short play. It's a story that is acted out in front of people. The people in the skit are called the characters. A skit can have one or more scenes. A scene shows an event in the story.

Skits can be about real events or make-believe events. When you write a skit, you write what the characters in the skit say and do. Look at the beginning of this skit about the Boston Tea Party.

The Boston Tea Party

Scene 1

Characters:

Members of the British Parliament

Setting:

At a Parliament meeting in Britain, 1773

Member 1: We've thought of a plan. Because the East India Company is having a hard time selling its tea here in Britain, let's ship the tea to the American colonies.

Member 2: We can sell this tea at a lower price than other companies and still make the colonists pay a tea tax. Then our Parliament will keep the money from the tea tax.

Member 3: The colonists may not like our plan.

Member 1: Britain rules the American colonies. They MUST pay our taxes and do what we say. Surely they will buy the tea and pay the tax.

STEPS IN Writing a Skit

Use these steps to write a skit.

1 Organize the Events

List the events you want to have in your skit and put them in order. Then write which characters will be part of each event. You can organize your events and characters in a chart like the one below.

2 Decide on a Title

The title is the name of the skit. A skit is often named after the main characters or event in the play.

3 Tell the Scene Number

If you have more than one scene in your skit, then write the scene number.

Events	Characters	Scene in Skit
Members of British Parliament meet and decide to ship East India tea to American colonies with a tea tax	Members of British Parliament	Scene 1
Samuel Adams and other colonists meet to plan what they will do about the British tea	Samuel Adams and other colonists	Scene 2
Samuel Adams and other colonists go onto the guarded British ship and throw the tea overboard	Samuel Adams, British guards, and other colonists	Scene 3

4 List Characters and Setting

After the scene number, list each of the characters that will appear in the scene. Tell when and where the scene takes place.

5 Write the Dialogue

The dialogue is what each of the characters says in the scene. Write the character's name followed by the words he or she says. The words that the characters speak should tell the main idea and action of the scene.

6 Stage Directions

The stage directions are words that are not spoken but give extra information about the events in the skit. Put all stage directions in parentheses.

7 Review Your Skit

Revise and edit your draft. Read it out loud. Is it interesting? Does it make sense? Make any changes that you think will make your skit better. Check your spelling and punctuation. Make a clean copy.

8 Perform the Skit

Choose someone to read each character's lines. Before performing the skit, practice reading the lines with everyone in the skit. Make sure everyone knows what to do and say.

EXAMPLE OF **Writing a Skit**

Read the skit below. Look at the different parts of the skit.

Title → The Boston Tea Party

Scene number → *Scene 2*

Characters:

Samuel Adams

Several other colonists

List of characters

(*Several colonists, including Samuel Adams are in a room. They are very serious. Some look angry.*)

Setting:

A meeting room in Boston on December 16, 1773

← **Setting**

Samuel Adams: Gentlemen, I think we all agree that a problem sits in Boston Harbor. The East India Tea Company wants to sell 342 chests of tea tomorrow.

Colonist 1: The Parliament is not being fair. The price of the East India Company tea will put me out of business.

Colonist 2: They are also making us pay a tax on the tea.

Samuel Adams: Let's show them that we think it's unfair. I have an idea of what we can do with that tea.

Colonist 1: What did you have in mind?

Dialogue

(*Everyone steps together and Samuel Adams whispers his plan to the colonists.*) ← **Stage directions**

USE THIS SKILL

Write a Skit

Write Scene 3 of the skit about the Boston Tea Party. The information below can help you to get started.

The Boston Tea Party

Scene 3

Characters:

Samuel Adams

____

____

(The colonists are dressed as Mohawk Indians. They are tiptoeing on the ship.)

Setting:

____

(Chests can be seen on the ship.)

Samuel Adams:

(whispering)__________________________________

______________: ______________________________

TEST TIP

You may be asked how a character thinks or feels on a test. Look at lines that the character says. Also look at the stage directions to see what the character does.

Skill 28

HOW TO

Write a Summary

Exploring New Land

Can you imagine traveling across America without roads or cars? The explorers Lewis and Clark did. They also wrote about their trip.

When writing about their journeys, Lewis and Clark sometimes wrote a summary of what they did or where they traveled. A **summary** tells the main ideas of something. If you tell someone about a book you read, then you are making a summary. You don't reread the book to them. You just tell about the most important ideas of the book.

You can use the following steps to write a summary of a story.

1 Read Carefully

Read the story and ask questions as you read. What is this story about? Who are the important people? When and where did this story take place? The answers can help you find the story's main ideas.

2 Take Notes

Take notes as you read to help you organize the story's main ideas. Write down each main idea. It may help to write the main idea of each paragraph.

TIP A summary should be short but long enough to describe the main ideas of the story.

STEPS IN **Writing a Summary**

3 Write a Draft

Your summary should begin with the most important idea. Then include any other main ideas from the story that you think are important to have in your summary.

4 Revise and Edit

Read the draft of your summary. Check for errors. Make sure you didn't include unimportant details from the story. Check your spelling, capitalization, and punctuation. Then write a neat copy of your summary.

Main ideas

Notes

- The U.S. bought the Louisiana Territory in 1803.
- Lewis and Clark were hired to explore the territory.
- A fur-trader and his wife, Sacagawea, were guides who helped the group.
- In 1805, Lewis and Clark reached the Pacific Ocean.

EXAMPLE OF Writing a Summary

Read the following story. Think about what main ideas you might include in the summary.

Lewis and Clark

In 1803, the United States bought a large area of land called the Louisiana Territory. President Thomas Jefferson hired two men, Meriwether Lewis and William Clark to explore the new land. Jefferson also wanted to know what rivers would lead to the Pacific Ocean.

Lewis and Clark led a group of 45 men. Along the way, they hired a fur trader and his Native American wife, Sacagawea, to be their guides. In 1805, the group reached the Pacific Ocean. Their journey had been long and difficult.

Most important idea

Lewis and Clark

President Jefferson hired Lewis and Clark to explore the Louisiana Territory. Their guides, a fur trader and Sacagawea, helped them on their long journey. Lewis and Clark reached the Pacific Ocean in 1805.

USE THIS SKILL

Write a Summary

Read the story. Write a summary of the following story.

Sacagawea with Lewis and Clark

Sacagawea was a Native American woman of the Shoshone tribe. She was born around 1787. Sacagawea was about 17 years old when the explorers Lewis and Clark came to the village where she and her husband lived. Because they could both speak more than one language, they were hired by Lewis and Clark as guides. They traveled with Lewis and Clark for the next eight months. The group went from an area that is today in North Dakota all the way to the Pacific Ocean. Sacagawea carried her infant son with her during the journey, making him America's youngest explorer.

TEST TIP

On a test, you may have to pick a sentence that summarizes a reading. Choose the sentence that tells the most important idea of the reading.

Skill 29

HOW TO

Use the Internet

U.S. Presidents

Did you know that you can find information about all of the presidents of the United States without opening a book? You can do this by using the Internet.

The **Internet** is a network that lets computers share information. The Internet is like a huge library. Instead of books, the Internet has Web sites. A **Web site** is all of the words and images that a group shows on the Internet. There are many Web sites that have information about U.S. presidents.

Web sites are found using a computer.

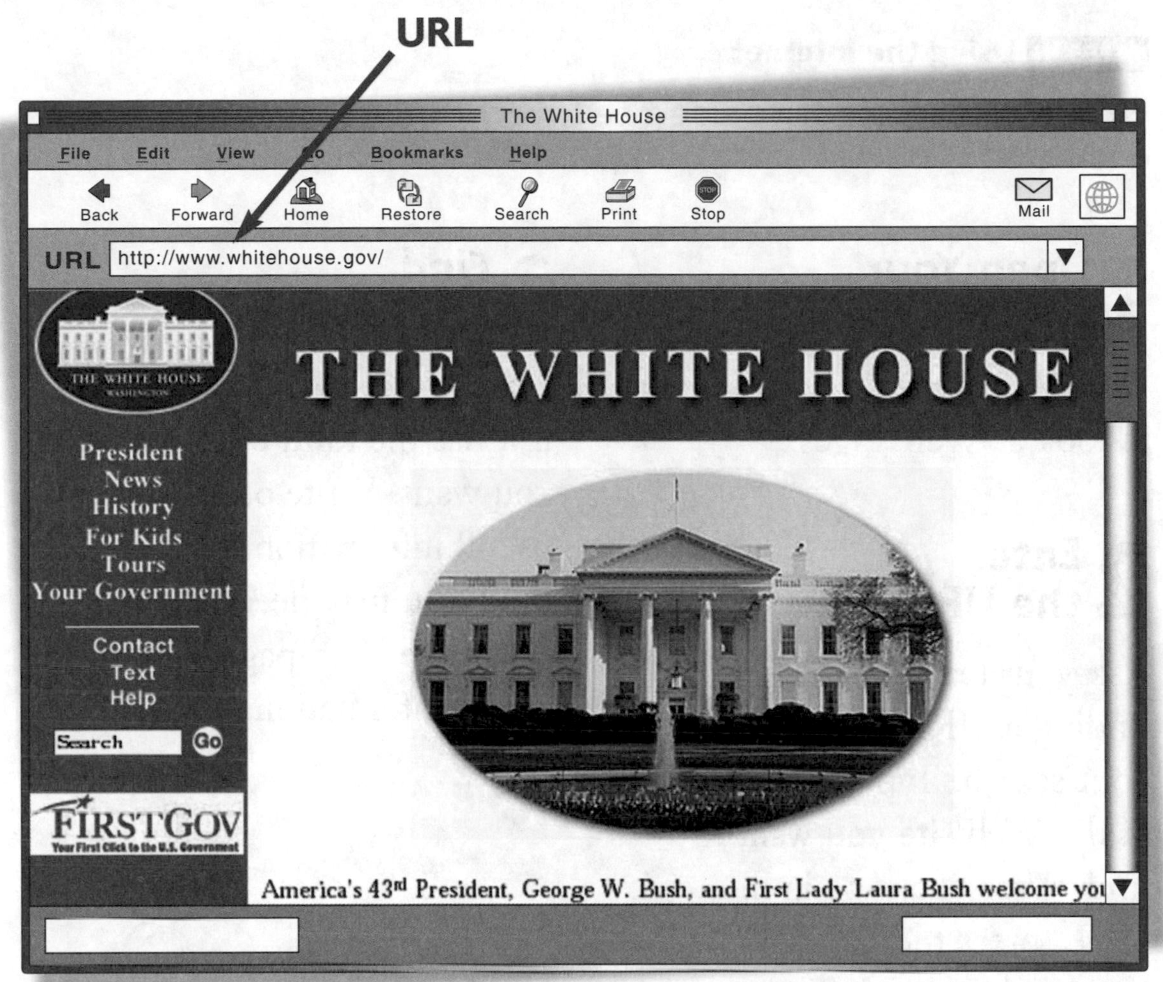

By looking at different Web sites, you can find information about our current president and past presidents. The Internet has millions of Web sites! Each Web site has a URL. URL stands for Uniform Resource Locator.

The URL is the address of a Web page. The URL tells your computer where to go for the information you want. A Web page is the information that you see on your computer screen when you enter a URL.

STEPS IN Using the Internet

Follow these steps to use the Internet.

1 Open Your Web Browser

Your Web browser allows you to look at Web pages.

2 Enter the URL

Ask your teacher for help in finding a URL and beginning your search. Type in the URL of the Web site you want to find. After you type in the URL, press the ENTER key on your keyboard. The computer will find your Web site and show you a Web page.

3 Find Information

Look at the Web page to see if it has the kind of information you want. Write or print the useful information that you find. You may need to scroll down the Web page to find useful information.

TIPS

- **URLs must be accurate in punctuation and spelling when typed.**
- **You can use the BACK and FORWARD buttons at the top of the computer screen to move between links.**

4 Record the URL

Remember to write down the URL of a Web page that had useful information. By recording the URL, you can go back to that Web page later. If you use the information in a report, then you will need to list the URL as the source of your information.

5 Find Links

Your Web page can lead you to many other Web pages. You may find that some words or phrases on the Web page are different colors and underlined. Each of these is a link to another Web page. Links can also be listed down the left side of the Web page or at the very bottom of the page. Click on the links to see if you can find more information about your topic.

Record the URL

EXAMPLE OF Using the Internet

Look at the information and links on the Web page below about past presidents of the United States. See what links and information you can find on this Web page.

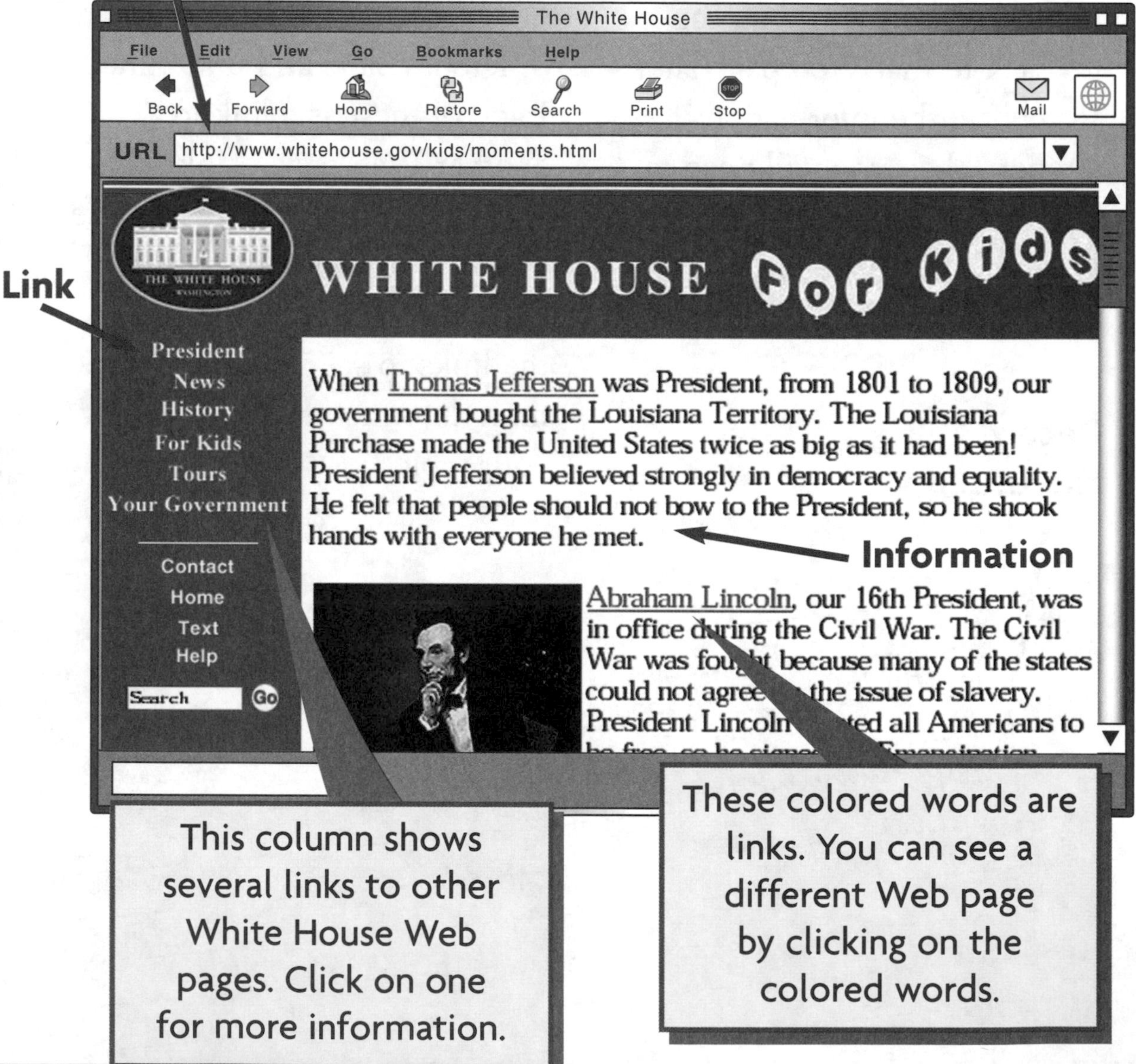

USE THIS SKILL

Use the Internet

Ask your teacher for a URL and answer the following questions about the Web page.

1. Who is talked about on this Web page?
2. What are three things you can learn about this person by reading the Web page?
3. What other people are discussed on the Web page?
4. Name two links on this page.
5. List two things that you would like to find out about the person on the Web page.

TEST TIP

Sometimes a test asks you to read a page to find the answers to questions. First take a quick look at the questions. Then read the passage. Go back to the passage to find the information you need.

Skill 30

HOW TO

Use Reference Sources

The Star-Spangled Banner

In 1814, the United States was at war. British troops had burned the White House and were traveling to Baltimore. To get to Baltimore, the British had to get past Fort McHenry.

On September 13, the British started bombing Fort McHenry. On a ship a few miles away, an American named Francis Scott Key watched the battle. At dawn, Key knew the Americans had won when he saw the U.S. flag flying over the fort. He was so happy that he wrote a poem called "The Star-Spangled Banner."

You can learn more about "The Star-Spangled Banner" by using reference sources. **Reference sources** are books or other sources that give information about a topic. One kind of reference source is an encyclopedia. An **encyclopedia** is a set of books with articles on many topics. Each book in the set is called a volume. Information is arranged in the volumes in ABC order by topic. The spine, or edge, of each volume is numbered and has letters to tell which part of the alphabet is in that volume. Follow the steps on the next page to use a reference source, such as an encyclopedia, to find information for a report.

STEPS IN Using Reference Sources

1 Choose a Topic

Decide what topic you want to learn about.

2 Identify Keywords

Think of keywords. Keywords are words that you can look up to learn about your topic, such as *Star-Spangled Banner* and *National Anthem*.

3 Look up Keywords

Pick a keyword and find its first letter on the spine of a volume. Open the volume and look at the words at the top of the page, called guide words. They help you find the article you want by showing the first entry words on the page. Entry words are the words in an article's title.

TIP Usually, words like **a, an,** and **the** will move to the end of an encyclopedia entry. For a topic like "The Star-Spangled Banner," look up the keyword **Star-Spangled** instead of **The.**

4 Take Notes

Write down the information you find useful in the article. At the end of each article, you can find a list of related topics that you can look up to find more information. Record the source of useful information by writing down the entry words (the article's title), the encyclopedia's name, the volume number, and the page number.

STAR-SPANGLED BANNER, THE,
Universe Encyclopedia, Volume 18,
page 421.

EXAMPLE OF **Using Reference Sources**

Read the article below and see how you can find information about "The Star-Spangled Banner" in an encyclopedia.

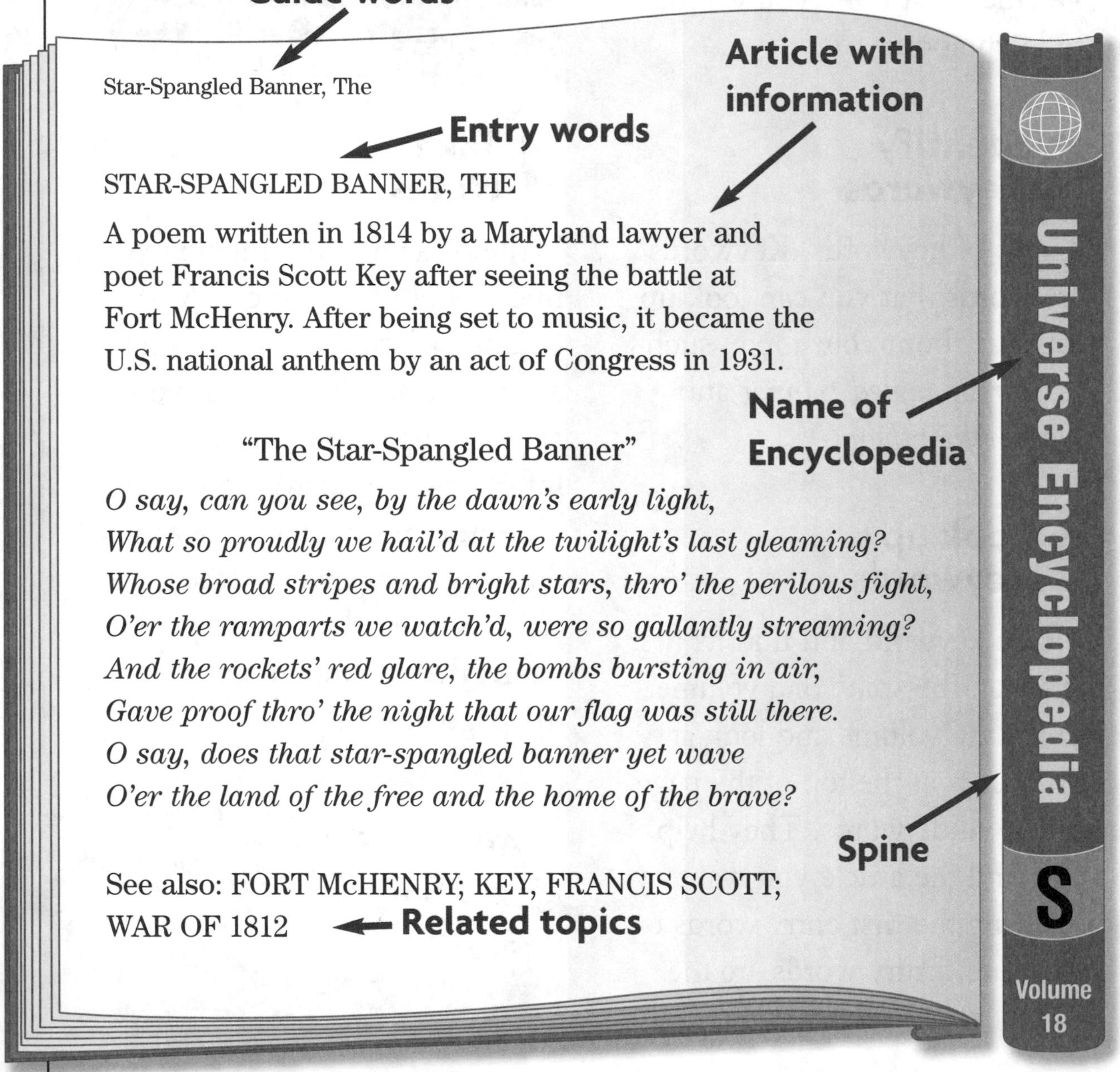

Guide words

Star-Spangled Banner, The

Article with information

Entry words

STAR-SPANGLED BANNER, THE

A poem written in 1814 by a Maryland lawyer and poet Francis Scott Key after seeing the battle at Fort McHenry. After being set to music, it became the U.S. national anthem by an act of Congress in 1931.

Name of Encyclopedia

"The Star-Spangled Banner"

O say, can you see, by the dawn's early light,
What so proudly we hail'd at the twilight's last gleaming?
Whose broad stripes and bright stars, thro' the perilous fight,
O'er the ramparts we watch'd, were so gallantly streaming?
And the rockets' red glare, the bombs bursting in air,
Gave proof thro' the night that our flag was still there.
O say, does that star-spangled banner yet wave
O'er the land of the free and the home of the brave?

Spine

See also: FORT McHENRY; KEY, FRANCIS SCOTT; WAR OF 1812 **Related topics**

Universe Encyclopedia

S

Volume 18

USE THIS SKILL

Use Reference Sources

Use one or more encyclopedias to find answers to the following questions.

1. Look up *Fort McHenry.* What are three things the encyclopedia tells about Fort McHenry?
2. Look up *Francis Scott Key.* When was he born and when did he die? What guide words were on the page where you found information about Francis Scott Key?
3. Look up the *War of 1812.* What are three things you can learn by reading the entry?
4. What are three keywords you would look up if you wanted to learn about the president that was in office the year that "The Star-Spangled Banner" was written?

TEST TIP

On a test, you may be asked to tell which reference source you would use to find an answer. Remember that different reference books have different information. Encyclopedias have articles on many topics. Dictionaries give word meanings. Atlases contain maps. An almanac has facts and figures on many topics.

Skill 31

HOW TO

Write an Outline

Virginia Plantations

In the 1700s, large farms in Virginia were places where fields were green and large crops were harvested. They were also places where people lived in slavery.

Virginia plantation

In the 1700s, many people in the southern United States lived on large farms. These large farms were called **plantations**. At this time, most of the people living on plantations were slaves. In the South, most slaves were from Africa or had families from Africa. The slaves were not given the rights or freedoms that people in America have today.

Virginia plantations were owned by white families. The people who worked as slaves on the plantations were thought of as property that belonged to the white plantation owners. Many of these people had been taken from their homes, sent away from their families, and forced into slavery.

Virginia Plantations

I. Size of Plantations
  A. More than 40,000 acres
  B. Less than 40,000 acres
II. Crops Grown on Plantations
  A. Tobacco
  B. Sugar
  C. Cotton
  D. Hemp

As you study slavery and plantation life in Virginia, you may want to organize the information you are learning. An **outline** is a list that organizes information by showing a topic, main ideas, and details.

When you make an outline, you write down the main ideas and details about the topic. The information in your outline will help your writing make sense and be better organized.

TIP In an outline, you can't have just one of a numeral, letter, or number. If you have a I, you must also have a II. If you have an A, you must also have a B.

STEPS IN Writing an Outline

Use the steps below to write an outline.

Main house of plantation

1 Identify the Topic

Write the topic of your outline at the top of your page. This is the title of your outline.

Example:

<u>Family Relationships</u>

2 Write the Main Ideas

A main idea tells about your topic. On the outline, write the main ideas in a word or short phrase. Use Roman numerals to number each of your main ideas.

Example:

I. Plantation Owners

II. Enslaved

3 Write Details

On the lines below each main idea, write details about that main idea. Indent each line and use capital letters for each detail that tells about the main idea.

TIP These are Roman numerals for the numbers 1–5.

I = 1	IV = 4
II = 2	V = 5
III = 3	

Family Relationships

I. Plantation Owners
- A. Close families
- B. Many family members in the main plantation house
- C. Marriage—husband and wife lived in same house

II. Enslaved
- A. Tried to have close families but family members could be sold at any time
- B. Close friends became a kind of family for many
- C. Marriage—husband and wife often lived on different plantations

EXAMPLE OF Writing an Outline

Read the sample outline. Can you tell what the topic of the outline is? Could you write a few paragraphs from this outline?

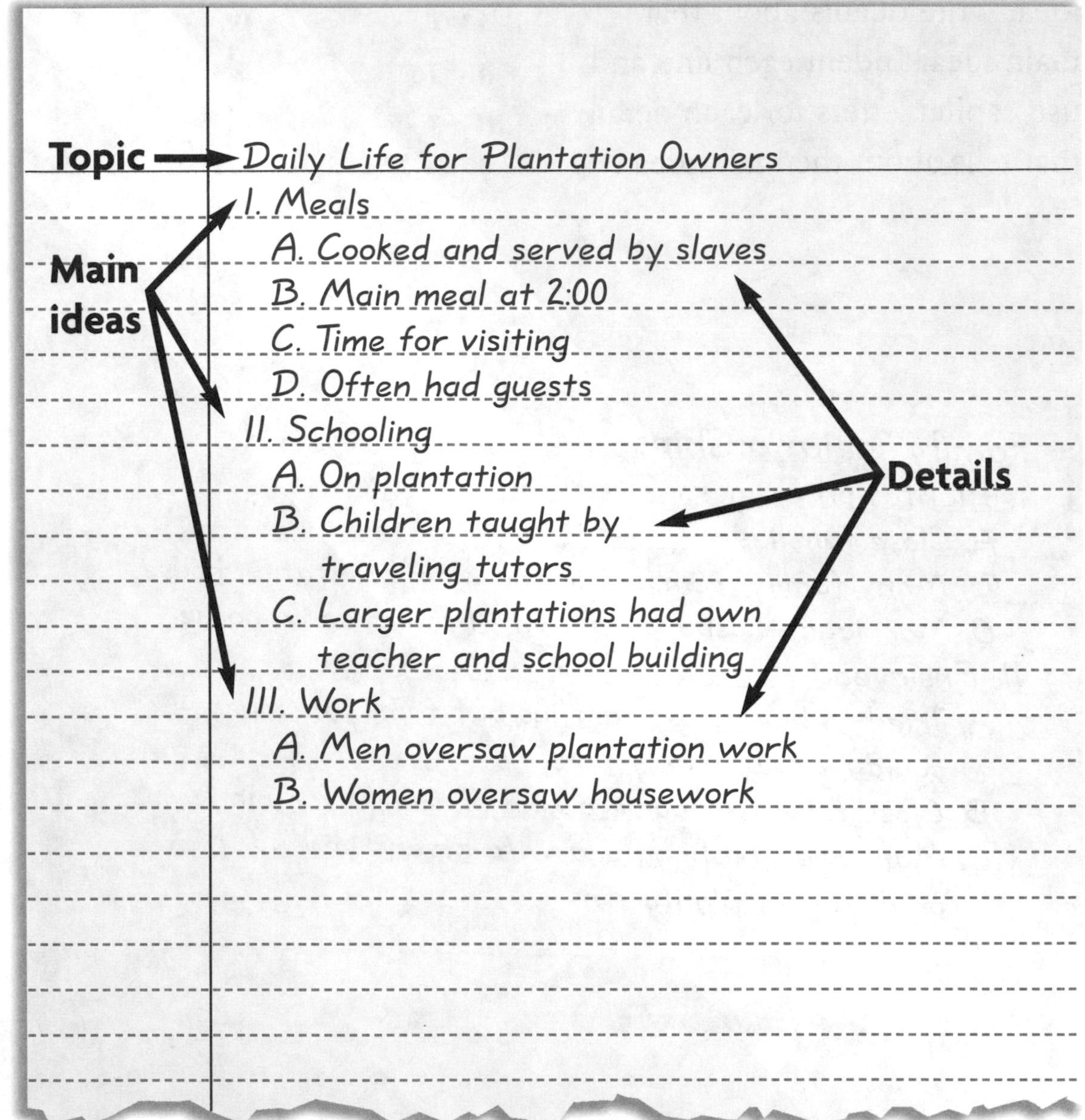

USE THIS SKILL

Write an Outline

Outline the information in the paragraphs below.

Daily Life for Plantation Slaves

Most of the work on a plantation was done by slaves. Daily life for plantation slaves centered around the work they did. Even though they worked hard year after year, they did not get paid.

Most slaves worked in the fields. Men, women, and even children began work early in the morning. They plowed, planted, cared for plants, and harvested.

Some slaves worked as house servants in the main house. They cooked, cleaned, served the white family, did laundry, sewed, and took care of the owner's children. House servants were often not able to see their friends or family who worked in the fields.

On larger plantations, some slaves learned trades and crafts. They worked as blacksmiths, carpenters, shoemakers, tailors, and midwives on the plantation.

TEST TIP

You may be asked to write an essay on a test. Before you begin writing, make an outline. When you write, follow your outline. This will make it easier to write the essay.

Skill 32

HOW TO

Write a Biography

Our First President

Do you know who the first president of the United States was? Our first president, George Washington, is still one of the United States' most honored leaders.

George Washington

In 1787, leaders from many states met at the Constitutional Convention in Philadelphia. Their main goal was to make a new national government and plan how it would work. They chose George Washington to lead the convention.

Some of the most important decisions made at the Constitutional Convention were about our nation's leader. Our leader would be called the president. The president would be elected by the people.

George Washington was elected as the first president of the United States of America in 1789. He is still the only president ever elected unanimously. This means that everyone voted for George Washington.

The Signing of the Constitution by Howard Chandler Christy

A **biography** is a story about a person's life. A biography can be written about anyone. You can learn a lot about history by reading biographies.

A biography about George Washington would tell you details about Washington's life. A biography would also tell you about the times during which he lived.

STEPS IN Writing a Biography

Use these steps to write a biography.

1 Choose Your Subject

Write about someone you know or would like to know. Think of a person who is interesting or inspiring to you.

George Washington, 1732–1799

2 Gather Information

Start by listing things you would like to know about the person. You can get information from books, magazines, the Internet, encyclopedias, and by talking to other people. Take notes on the information you find. List details that you find out about the person.

TIP **Record information about each source you use: title, author, publisher, copyright date, page numbers, or Internet addresses.**

3 Organize Your Information

Put your notes in an order that makes sense. You can make a time line to order the important events that happened in the person's life.

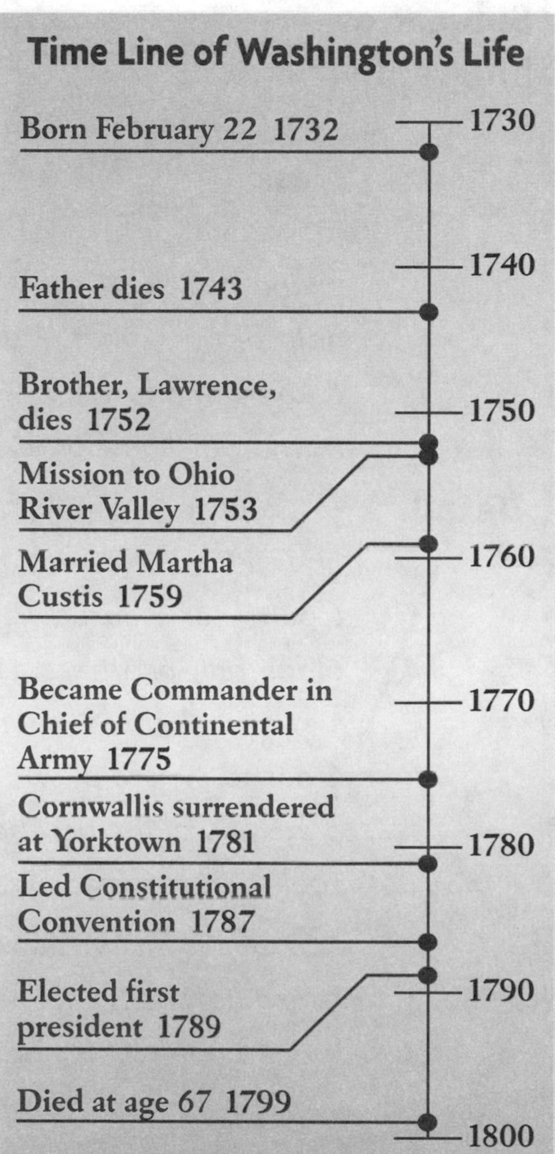

4 Write the Biography

Write a draft using your notes and time line. You might start with a quotation from the person. Include details about your subject's life to make the story interesting. You can order the information from the beginning to the end of your subject's life.

Revise and edit your draft. Read your draft. Make any changes that you think will make your biography better. Check your spelling and punctuation. Make a final copy of your biography.

EXAMPLE OF Writing a Biography

Read the sample biography of George Washington.

Subject of biography → *George Washington*

When George Washington was elected president, no one knew for sure what the job would be like. The United States was brand-new. George Washington would help define what a president is and does. Maybe that's why he is known as "The Father of His Country." ← **Quote**

Details

George Washington had many brothers and sisters. He was born in Westmoreland County on February 22, 1732. He had two older half-brothers. He also had a younger sister and three younger brothers. When George was eleven years old, his father died. His older brother Lawrence then took care of George.

Education was very important to the Washingtons. The two older brothers were sent to school in England. George went to school in Virginia. Many of the things he studied helped him become a great officer and president.

USE THIS SKILL

Write a Biography

Pick a president from the chart below and write a short biography about his life. Write at least two or three paragraphs.

Early Presidents of the United States		
Name	*Term*	*Nickname*
John Adams	1797–1801	Atlas of Independence
Thomas Jefferson	1801–1809	Man of the People Sage of Monticello
James Madison	1809–1817	Father of the Constitution
John Quincy Adams	1825–1829	Old Man Eloquent
Andrew Jackson	1829–1837	Old Hickory

TEST TIP

You may be asked to write about a person on a test. Tell about the important things the person did. Write so your reader will understand the person.

Skill 33

HOW TO

Prepare an Oral Report

Women of the Revolutionary War

Did you know that women played an important role in America's fight for freedom? Women were soldiers, messengers, builders, writers, nurses, and caretakers.

Cannon

To learn about women in the Revolutionary War, you can read books about them. You can also tell about a book you've read by giving an oral report. An **oral report** is a spoken report that shares information about a subject. When you give an oral report you tell important facts and share your personal feelings about your subject.

An oral report has three main parts: a beginning, a middle, and an end. Each part is important so that people understand your topic and are interested in your report.

Molly Cochran Corbin

The beginning of your report names your subject and gets your audience interested.

The middle of your report gives important facts about your subject.

The end of your report tells why your subject is important to you and others.

Read this introduction to a book report.

Most books tell about George Washington and Paul Revere in their chapters on the American Revolution. These men were very important in the war but they weren't alone. Many people were part of the revolution. Molly Cochran Corbin is just one of many revolutionary heroines.

STEPS IN Preparing an Oral Report

Use these steps to prepare an oral report.

1 Find Your Topic

Think of a person or event that is interesting or inspiring to you. Read a book or other materials to learn about your person or event. Take notes to help you remember important facts.

2 Organize Information

Think about what you want to say in the beginning, middle, and ending. Begin your report with something that will interest the audience. The middle of the report should give information, such as facts and your feelings, about your topic. End your report by telling what you learned or why your topic is important.

Notes

Molly Cochran Corbin

- Went with husband when he joined the war
- Worked in the military camps
- Fought the British when her husband was killed
- She was shot by the British

Things to Remember
1. Speak slowly and clearly.
2. Speak loudly so everyone can hear.
3. Stand up straight and try not to fidget.
4. Look up. If you don't want to look directly at someone, look just above your listeners' heads.
5. Keep going even if you make a mistake.

3 Practice Your Report

Practice giving your report a few times. You might want to practice in front of a mirror or record yourself. Remember to talk slowly and clearly. Be sure you know how to say all the words correctly.

4 Give Your Report

Use any props that will make your report more interesting. Props are visual aids that can help you show your listeners information about your topic. Look up at your classmates. Do not talk too fast.

EXAMPLE OF Preparing an Oral Report

Read this book report aloud.

Beginning

Molly Cochran Corbin

During the Revolutionary War, there were some women in the Continental army. Most of them were known as "camp followers." Camp followers took care of many jobs in the army camps. They cooked, cleaned, mended clothes, helped set up and tear down camps, and took care of the wounded.

Middle

Margaret "Molly" Corbin was a camp follower. When her husband joined the Continental army, Molly went with him. Along with the other women, Molly took care of the camp and the soldiers in it. The work was hard and the women did not get paid.

During the Battle of Fort Washington, Molly's husband was shot. When Molly saw him fall to the ground, she ran out onto the battlefield to help him. It was too late. Molly's husband was dead. Molly took the place of her husband and helped fire a cannon at the British until she was shot. Molly Corbin survived the shooting. Her care and courage in the Revolutionary War are still remembered.

End →

USE THIS SKILL

Prepare an Oral Report

Pick a woman from the chart below. Read the book listed by her name or another book about her and prepare an oral report.

Women of the Revolutionary War	
Name	*Book*
Molly Pitcher	*Molly Pitcher: Young Patriot* by Augusta Stevenson
Wyn Mabie	*Daughter of Liberty: A True Story of the American Revolution* by Robert Quackenbush
Deborah Sampson	*The Secret Soldier: The Story of Deborah Sampson* by Ann McGovern
Sybil Ludington	*Sybil Ludington's Midnight Ride* by Marsha Amstel
Phyllis Wheatley	*Phyllis Wheatley* by Victoria Sherrow
Betsy Ross	*Betsy Ross* by Alexandra Wallner

TEST TIP

On a test, you may be asked to write a story. Think about the beginning, middle, and end of the story before you start writing. This will help you write a story that makes sense.

Chart and Graph Skills

Skill 34

HOW TO

Read a Time Line

Incredible Inventions

How would your day be different if there were no telephones, computers, or televisions? Many inventions have changed the lives of people in the United States.

Some things were invented a long time ago. Others were invented this year. To show when things were invented, you could use a time line. A **time line** is a line that shows the order in which events happened. A time line also shows how much time passed between two or more events.

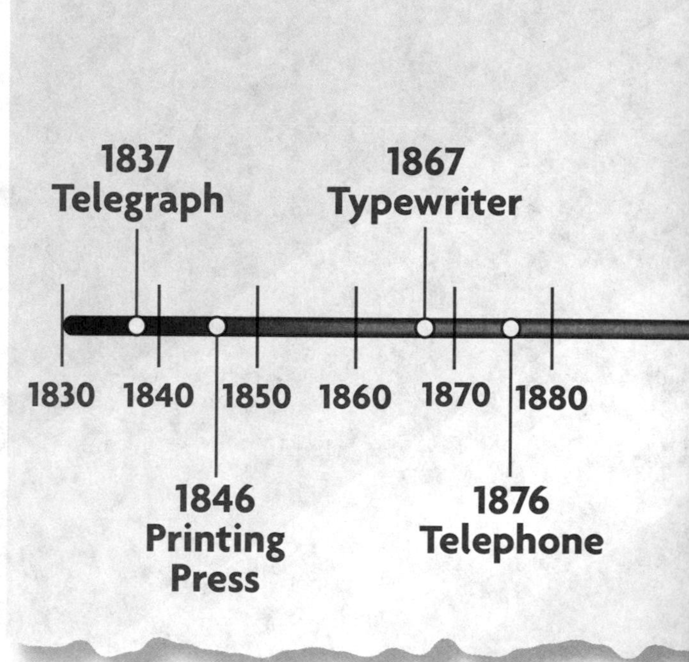

Time lines can show different amounts of time. One time line may show what happened over many years. Another may show what happened during a day.

The first event is at the left of the time line. The last event is at the right of the time line. The events on the left happened before the events on the right.

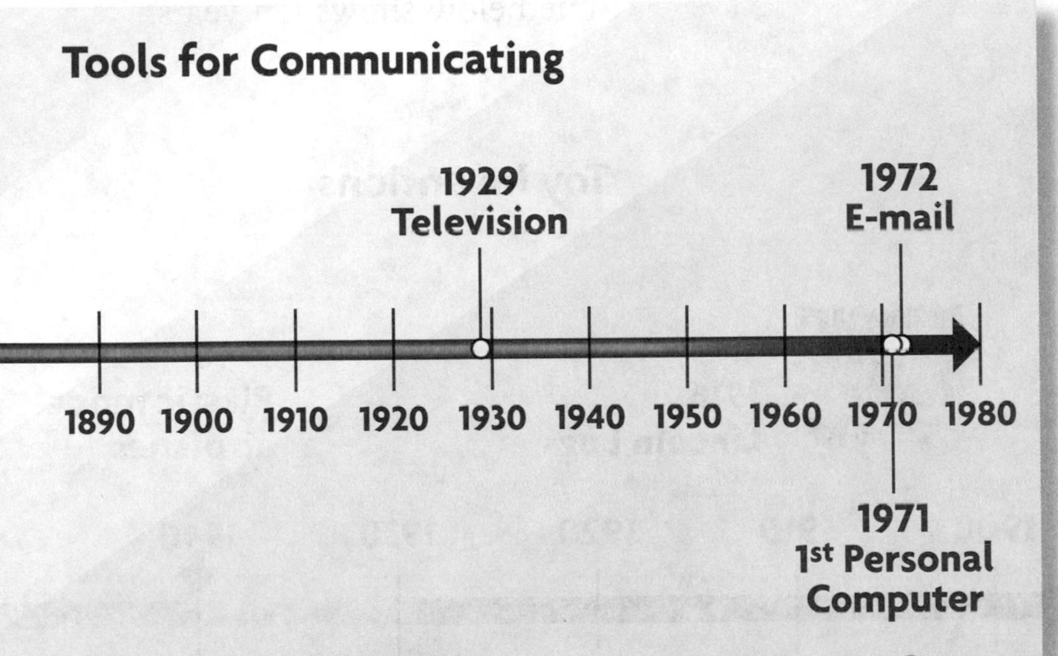

TIP To find the time that passed between two events, subtract the earlier date from the later date.

Example: 1972–1949 = 23 years

STEPS IN **Reading a Time Line**

1 Read the Title

The title of the time line will tell you how the events are related to each other.

2 Divided Time

Time lines are divided into equal parts. Find how many years each part of the time line shows. Each part of the time line below shows ten years.

Toy Inventions

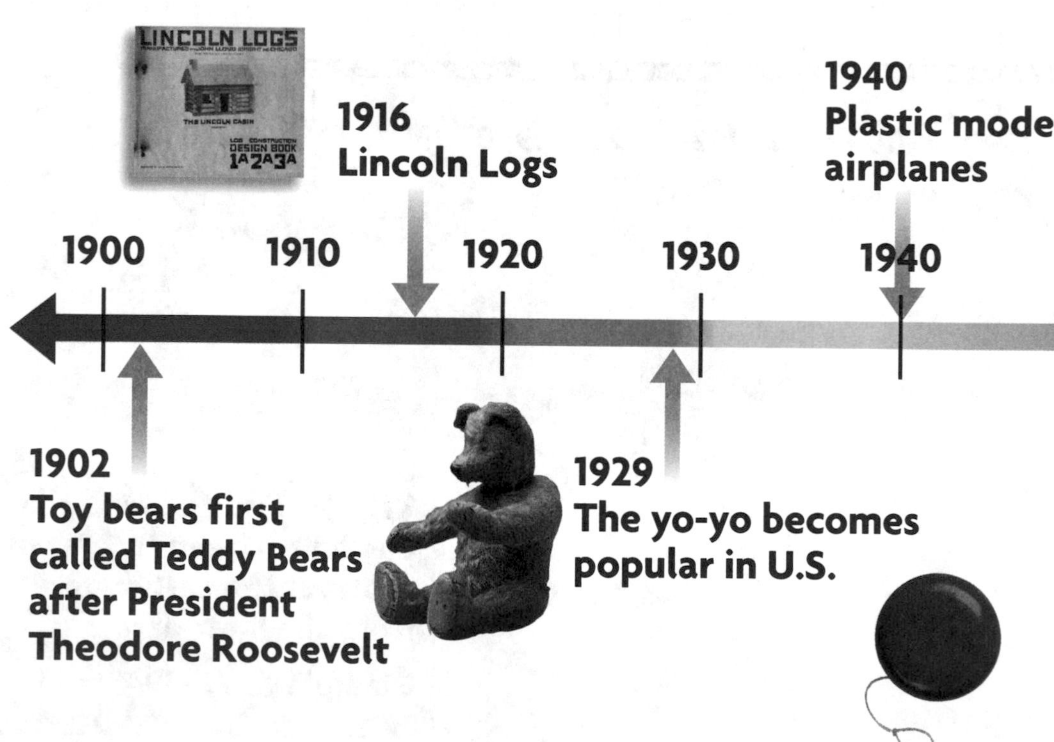

3 Find the Time

Find out the amount of time shown on the time line. Look for the first and last dates on the time line.

4 Look Between Events

Read the events from left to right on the time line. Note how much time passes between each event.

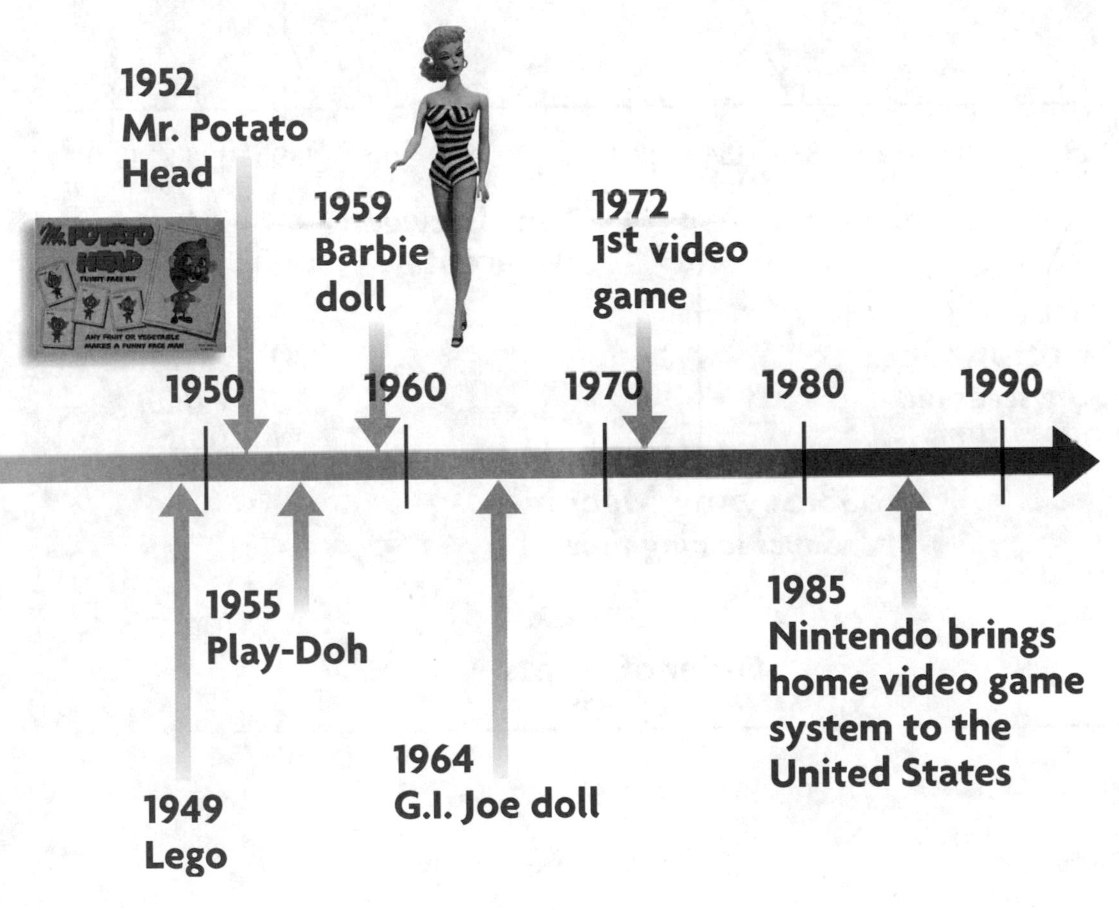

EXAMPLE OF Reading a Time Line

Read the following time line.

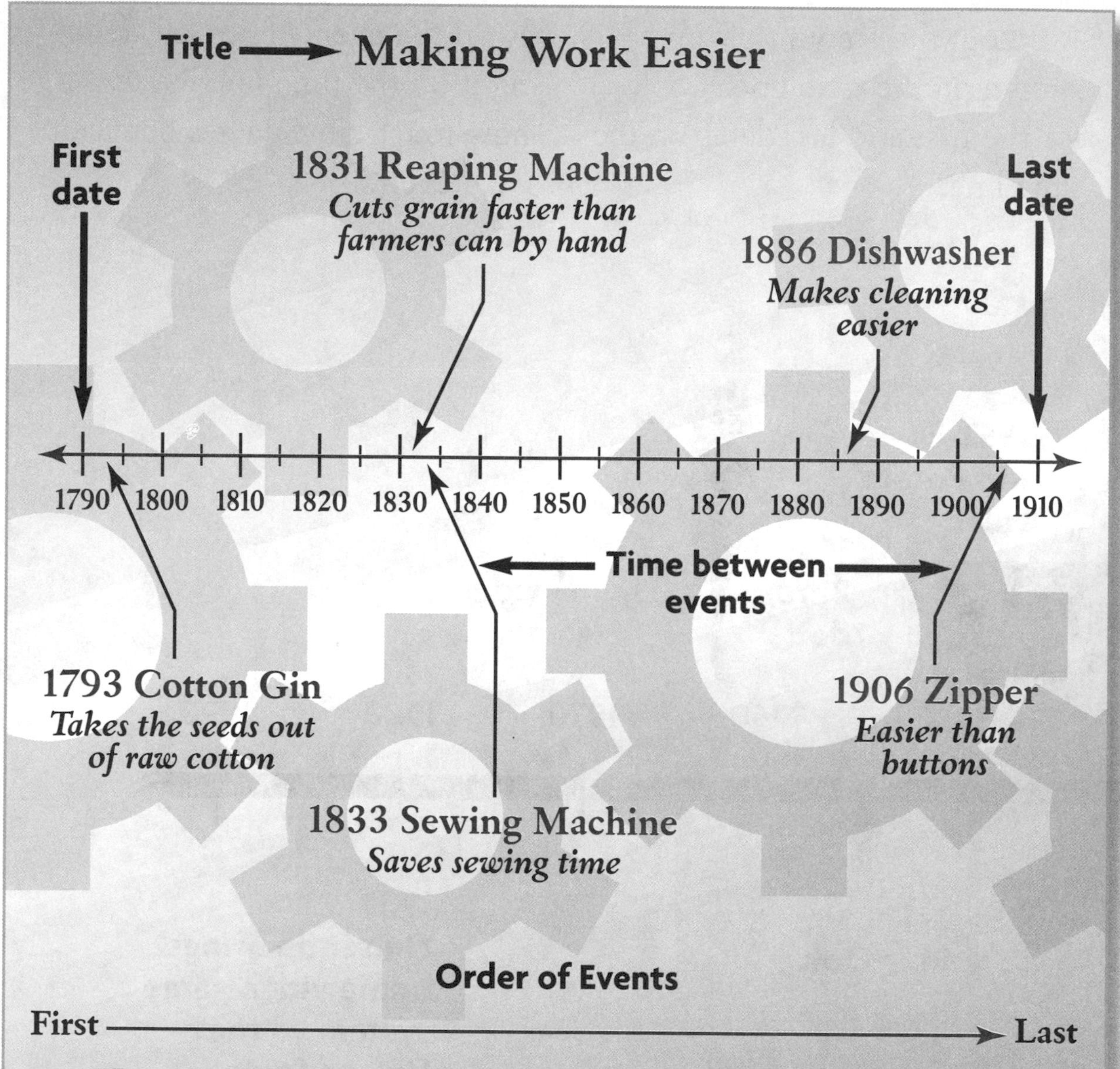

USE THIS SKILL

Read a Time Line

Read the time line and answer the following questions.

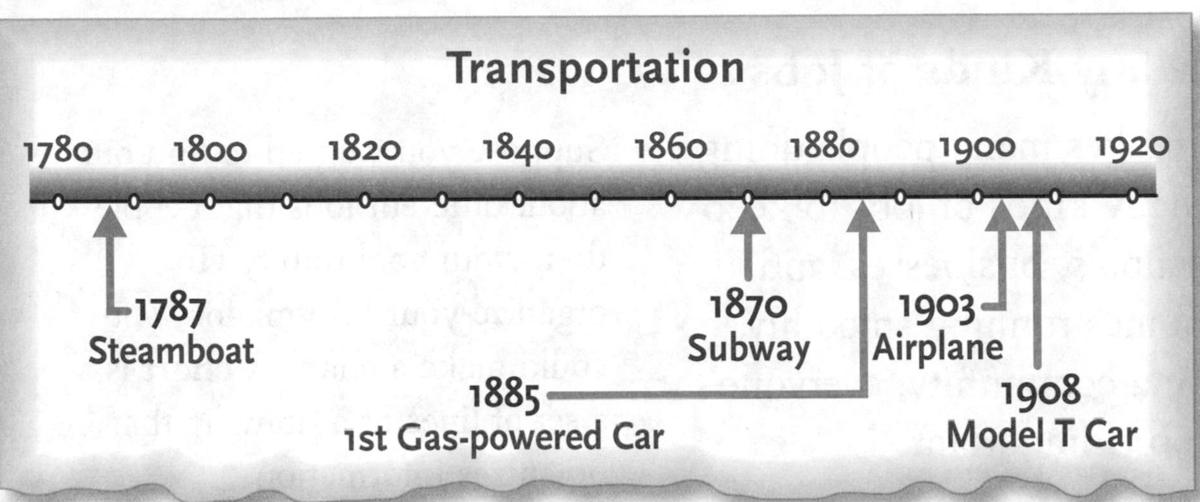

1. What is the title of the time line?
2. When was the first gas-powered car invented?
3. How much time passed between the invention of the steamboat and the subway?
4. Which came first, the airplane or the subway?
5. What is the last invention shown on the time line?

TEST TIP	You may be asked to tell which event happened first by reading a time line. Remember the events on the left happened before the events on the right on a time line.

Skill 35

HOW TO

Make a Chart

Many Kinds of Jobs

It takes many people doing many kinds of jobs to keep schools, businesses, and homes running smoothly. In a community, everyone's job is important.

A **job** is the work that a person does. Jobs provide goods or services that people need or want. In a community, everyone depends on workers with different kinds of jobs. If every person were a teacher, for example, there would be no one to give medical care, fix broken pipes, or drive school buses. Each kind of job is important.

Suppose you wanted to find out about different jobs that people do in your community. To organize your information, you could make a chart. A **chart** is a set of lines or a drawing that organizes information.

A chart can help you compare information. Charts also help you show a lot of information so it's easy to read. Read the steps on the following page to learn how to make a chart.

STEPS IN Making a Chart

1 Title the Chart

Look over the information you gathered. Think of a few simple words that describe the information. Use these words as the title of your chart.

2 Sort Your Information

A chart has columns and rows. Columns go down the chart. Rows go across the chart. In the first column, list the items that you want to compare. Label the top of each column with a word or two that describes the information that will go in each column.

3 Fill in the Chart

Fill in the chart by listing the details about each item. The details should describe the item at the left of the row as well as the words at the top of the column.

Column

Community Jobs

Job	Main Activity
Grocery store owner	Sells groceries
Police officer	Enforces laws
Teacher	Teaches students
Travel agent	Arranges trips
Janitor	Cleans buildings
Car dealer	Sells cars
Farmer	Grows food

Row →

Detail

EXAMPLE OF Making a Chart

Read the chart below. Think about how the chart shows information about the people in the neighborhood and the jobs that each person does.

Column

Title

Row

People's Jobs in My Neighborhood

Job	Main Activity	Name
Banker	Lends money	Kyra McKenzie
Baby-sitter	Cares for children	Tiffany Logan
Car mechanic	Fixes cars	Jim Ellis
Gas station owner	Sells gasoline	Irene Lewinski
Librarian	Keeps track of public books	Michael Lin
Dentist	Cares for teeth	Rashid Aryia

Items being compared

Details

USE THIS SKILL

Make a Chart

Make a chart by organizing the information from the paragraph into the chart.

People do many different jobs in our community. Ms. Johnson is a saxophonist. She plays the saxophone in a jazz band and performs all over the country. Mr. Witz is an electrician. He puts electrical wiring in homes. Ms. Lupinski is a hospital clerk. She takes care of patients' medical records. Mr. Kim is a music-store owner. He sells CDs.

Jobs in Our Community

Job	Main activity	Name
Saxophonist		Ms. Johnson
	Takes care of patients' medical records	
Music store owner		Mr. Kim

TEST TIP Some tests ask you to read charts. Lay a ruler or a piece of paper over part of the chart to help you read the information in the column or row that is asked about in the question.

Skill 36

HOW TO

Make a Bar Graph

Where Was It Made?

Did you know that many of the things that you use and wear were made in another country? Americans buy many things that are made by people in the United States and other countries.

When you make something like a toy or car, you are manufacturing. You **manufacture** when you make something by putting materials together by hand or with a machine. Many things are manufactured in the United States and other countries around the world.

Chart

Things Made	
Items	**Amounts**
Cookies	7
T-shirts	10
Cakes	2
Artwork	4

If you want to show information about what things are manufactured, you can make a bar graph. A **bar graph** is a kind of drawing that uses rectangles called bars to show information. Bar graphs can help you compare two or more things. Use the steps on the next page to make a bar graph using information from a chart.

1 List Items and Numbers

List the items in the chart under the bottom line of the graph. At the left side of the graph, make a number scale by listing numbers starting at the bottom with 0 and ending at the top with the largest number in the chart. Draw a line by each number. Each bar on a bar graph stands for a number. A bar stands for the number on the number scale that is even with the top of the bar.

2 Make the Bars

Make a bar for each item on the graph. Each bar should be a rectangle that matches the amount listed in the chart.

3 Title and Label the Graph

Above the bar graph, write a title that tells what the graph shows. Write a label to describe the information you have on each side of the graph.

EXAMPLE OF Making a Bar Graph

Look at the bar graph below. Think about how the bar graph shows the information in the chart.

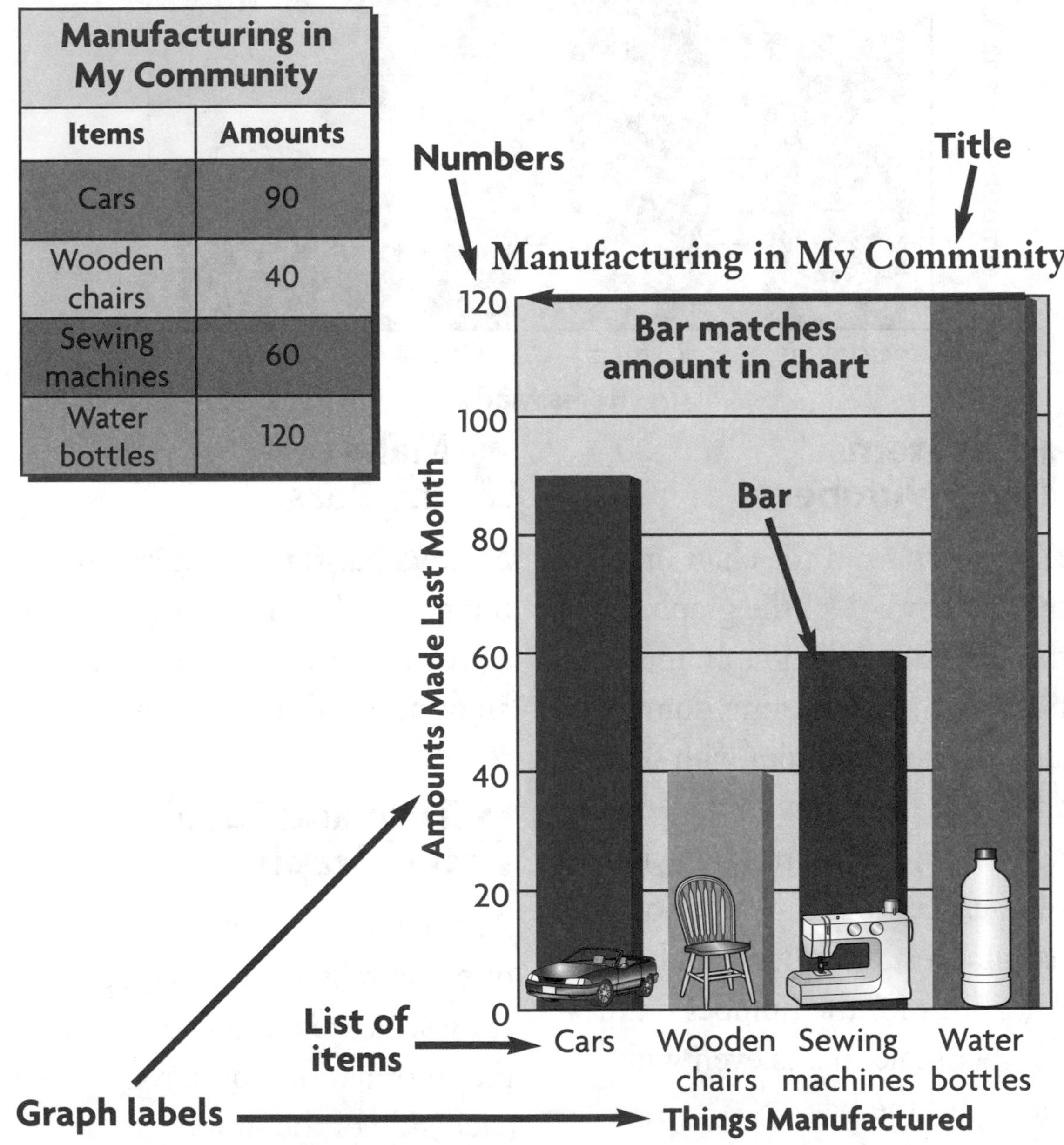

Manufacturing in My Community	
Items	**Amounts**
Cars	90
Wooden chairs	40
Sewing machines	60
Water bottles	120

USE THIS SKILL

Make a Bar Graph

Make a bar graph that shows the information in the chart below.

Countries Where My Shirts Were Manufactured	
Country	**Number of Shirts**
China	3
U.S.A.	4
Canada	1
Mexico	2

TEST TIP

You may be asked to read a bar graph on a test. Remember that longer bars stand for larger numbers and shorter bars stand for smaller numbers.

Skill 37

HOW TO

Make a Line Graph

Henry Ford and the Assembly Line

Can you imagine the United States without cars? It wasn't until the late 1800s that cars began moving on American roads.

The first cars took a long time to make and cost a lot of money. In 1913, an American car maker named Henry Ford found a way to build cars more quickly and cheaply. He made cars on a moving assembly line. A moving **assembly line** is a way of making something by having the item being made move along a path to workers who build certain parts.

Workers on Ford's assembly line

On Ford's assembly line, one set of workers would put on the car doors and another would put in the engines. The cars were made quickly by having workers do the same job on each car. The cars cost less money to make so they cost less money to buy, which let more people buy cars.

STEPS IN **Making a Line Graph**

To show the number of cars Ford sold over time, you could make a line graph. A **line graph** is a kind of drawing that uses a line to show how something changes over time. Use these steps to make a line graph using information from a chart.

1 Make Time and Number Scales

List the dates or times from the chart under the bottom line of the graph. Along the left side of the graph, list numbers from 0 to the largest number in the chart. Put a small line by each date and number.

Making Ford Cars	
Date	Amounts
1915	1 million
1924	10 million
1927	15 million

2 Draw the Points and Line

Find the place where each pair of numbers and dates from the chart meets on the graph. Make a point, or dot, on this place. After you make all of the points, connect them with a line.

3 Title and Label the Graph

Above the line graph, write a title that tells what the graph shows. Write a label to describe the information you have on each side of the graph.

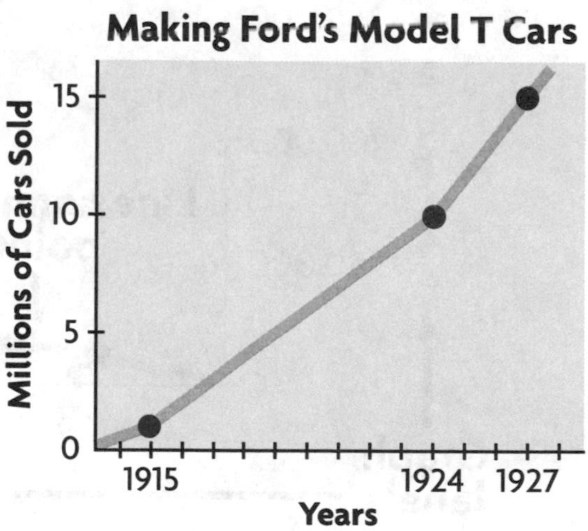

EXAMPLE OF **Making a Line Graph**

Look at the parts of the line graph below. See how the line graph shows how many more cars Ford made after he began his moving assembly line in 1913.

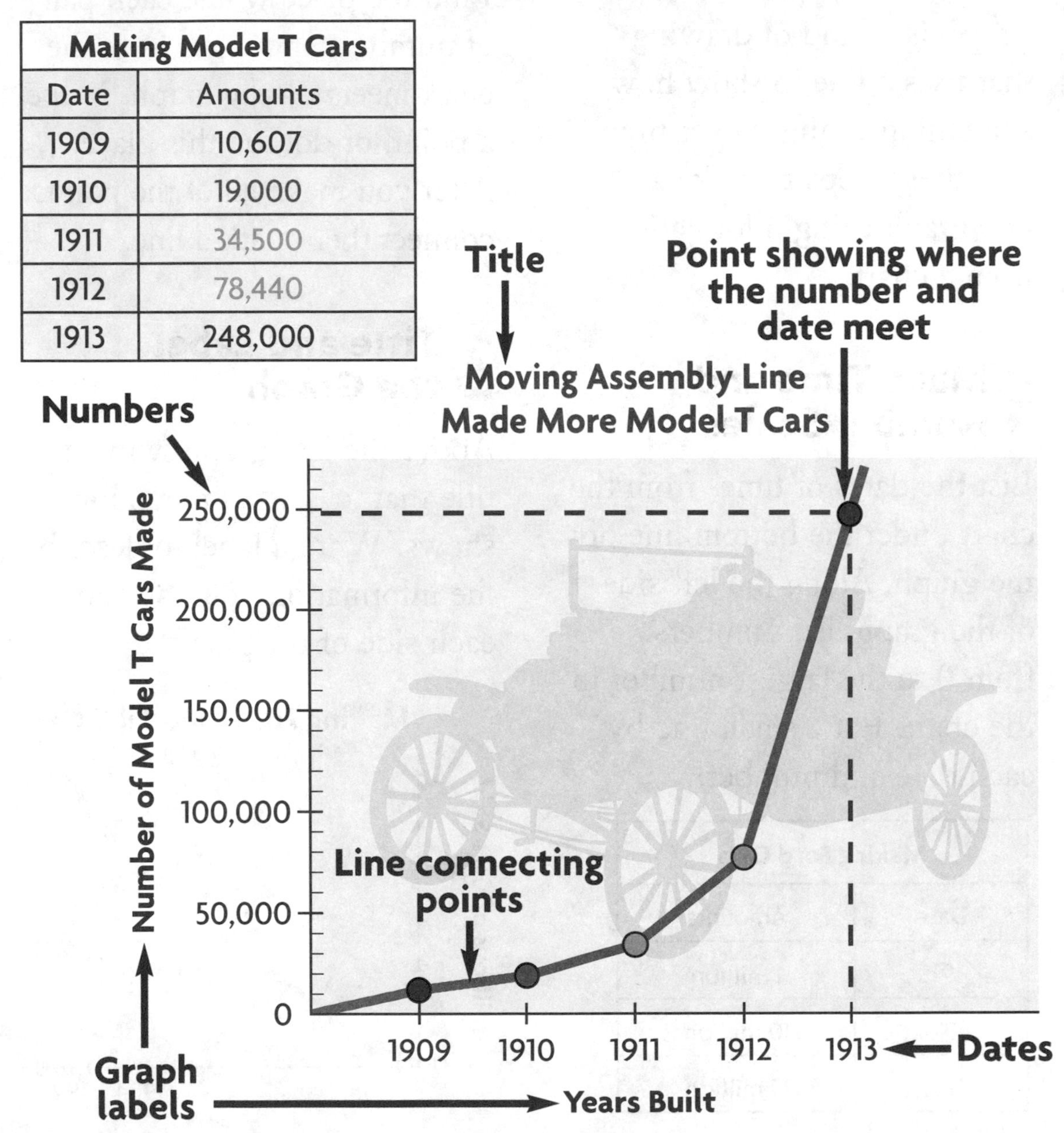

Making Model T Cars	
Date	Amounts
1909	10,607
1910	19,000
1911	34,500
1912	78,440
1913	248,000

USE THIS SKILL

Make a Line Graph

Read the passage below. Then use the information in the chart to make a line graph.

Henry Ford's Dream

Henry Ford's assembly line allowed Ford to cut the price of his most popular model of car, the Model T. In 1909, the Model T sold for about $1,000. By 1920, the price was cut to $355. In 1925, the price was down to $300. A lower price meant that more people could afford to buy the Model T. Ford was on his way to making his dream of "putting America on wheels" come true.

Model T

Cost of the Model T	
Date	**Price**
1909	$1,000
1920	$355
1925	$300

TEST TIP **You may be asked to read a line graph on a test. Remember that the higher the line goes on a graph, the larger the number it represents.**

Skill 38

HOW TO

Read a Diagram

The Three Branches of Government

Did you know that our government has many parts that work together? A diagram can show how our government works.

A **diagram** is a drawing that shows the parts of something. A diagram can show how parts fit together or how something works. Look at the diagram below to see the three branches, or parts, of our government.

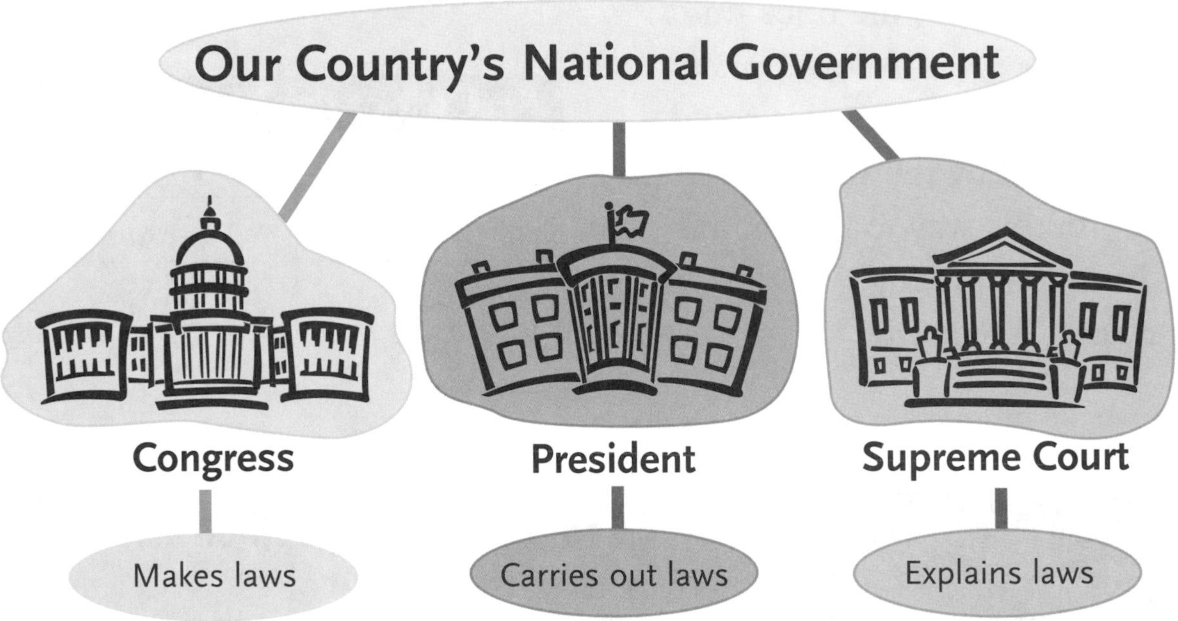

Our Country's National Government

Congress	President	Supreme Court
Makes laws	Carries out laws	Explains laws

STEPS IN **Reading a Diagram**

There are many kinds of diagrams that show the parts of something. A picture diagram uses photos or drawings. A line diagram uses only words and lines. Different diagrams can show information differently. Use the following steps to read a diagram.

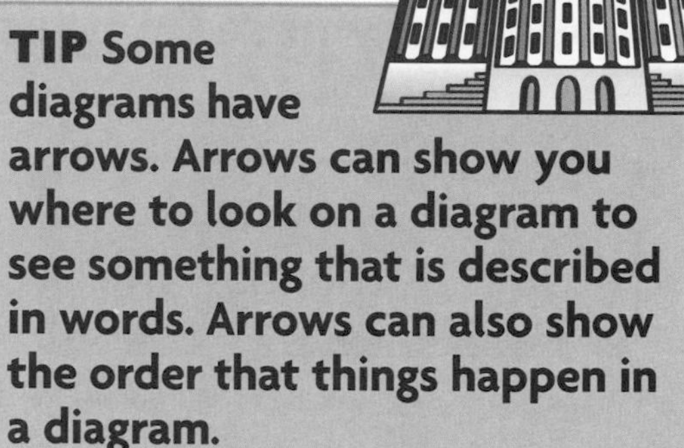

TIP Some diagrams have arrows. Arrows can show you where to look on a diagram to see something that is described in words. Arrows can also show the order that things happen in a diagram.

1 Look at Lines and Pictures

Be sure to look at the whole diagram. The lines on a diagram can show how information on the diagram is connected. The pictures can show details.

2 Read the Title

The title tells the topic of the diagram. Titles are often at the top of the diagram.

3 Read Any Captions

Captions are different from titles. They are usually under the diagram. A caption tells the relationships being shown in the diagram.

4 Read All Labels

Labels tell you the names of the small parts of the diagram.

EXAMPLE OF **Reading a Diagram**

Look at the diagram below to see the U.S. Capitol, the building where Congress works.

The title tells the topic of the diagram.

Labels tell you the names of the small parts of the diagram.

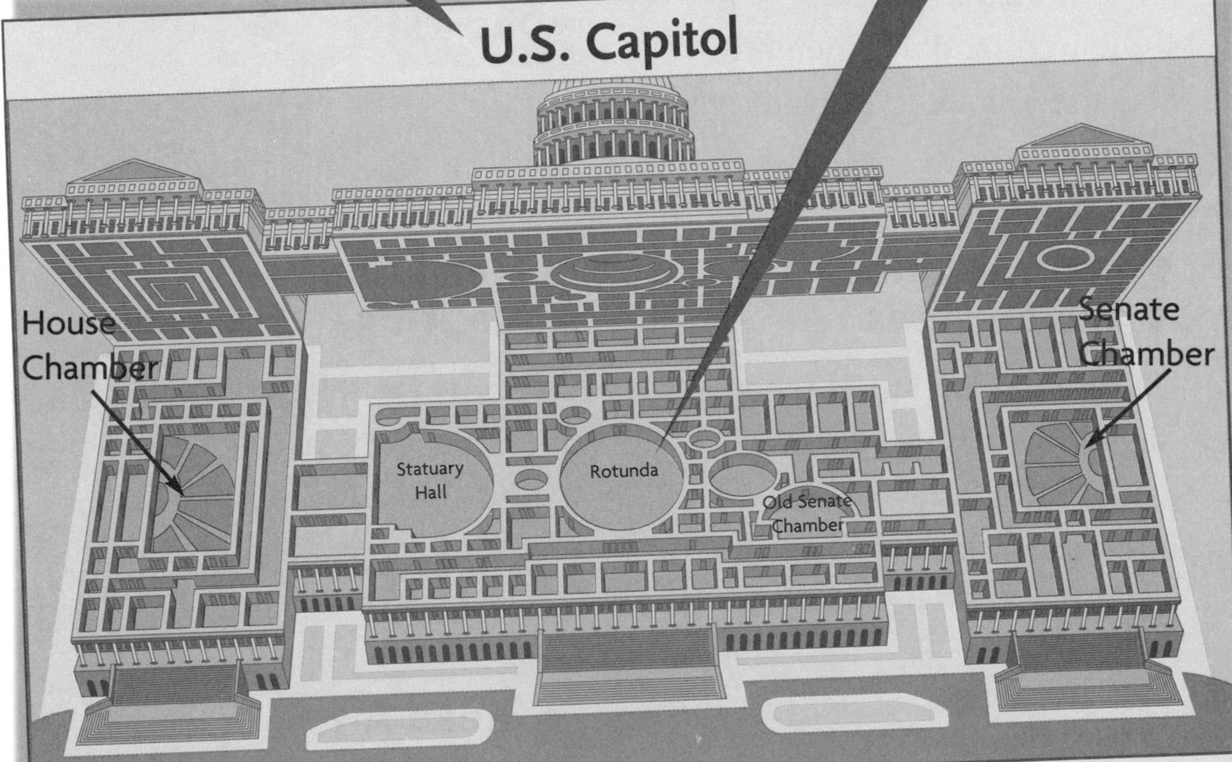

Congress works in the U.S. Capitol. Congress is made up of the House of Representatives and the Senate. These groups meet in different rooms, or chambers.

The caption tells the relationships being shown in the diagram.

USE THIS SKILL

Read a Diagram

Look at the diagram below and answer the following questions.

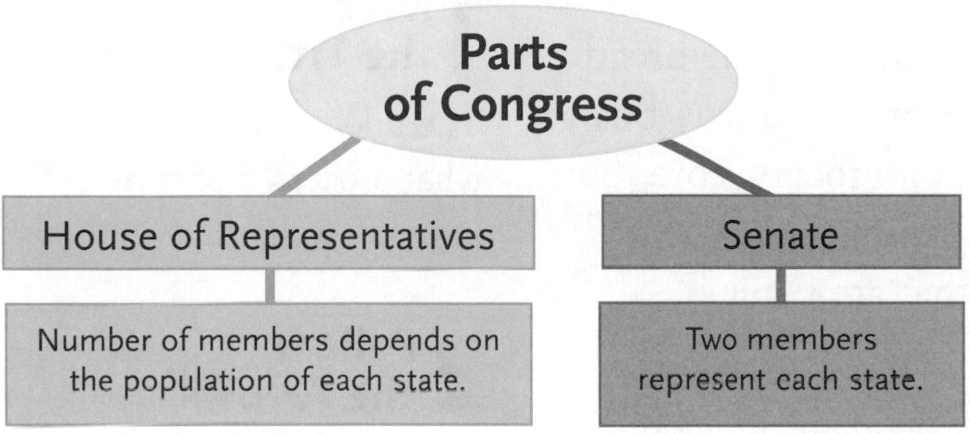

1. What is the title of the diagram?
2. What are the two parts of Congress?
3. What is different about the two parts of Congress?
4. How is this diagram similar to and different from the diagram on page 190?

TEST TIP **You may be asked to read a diagram on a test. Skim the diagram, then read the questions. Look back at the diagram to find the answers.**

Skill 39

HOW TO Read a Flowchart

From Seed to Sandwich

Do you know where bread comes from? You may buy bread at a grocery store, but bread begins with wheat seeds that are planted in soil.

Bread is an important food for many people. If you wanted to see how bread is made, you could look at a flowchart. A **flowchart** is a kind of drawing that shows the steps in a process. It can be made of pictures, words, or boxes. A flowchart has arrows to show you the order of the steps. Use the following steps to read a flowchart.

1 Read the Title

The title will tell you what process is shown in the flowchart.

2 Follow the Arrows

As you read the flowchart, look for the arrows that connect each part. Follow the direction of the arrows to find out the order of each step in the process.

TIP Using your finger to trace the arrows on the flowchart may help you to follow the order of the steps.

STEPS IN **Reading a Flowchart**

How Wheat is Grown

1. Plowing
Soil is made ready.

2. Sowing
Seeds are planted.

3. Harvesting
Wheat plants are gathered.

3 Look at the Pictures

Look at any pictures that are shown in the flowchart. The pictures can give more information about a step in the process. Pictures may show how or where part of the process is done.

4 Read All Labels

The labels on the flowchart will give you details about the steps that are shown on the flowchart.

EXAMPLE OF Reading a Flowchart

Look at the flowchart below to see how bread is made.

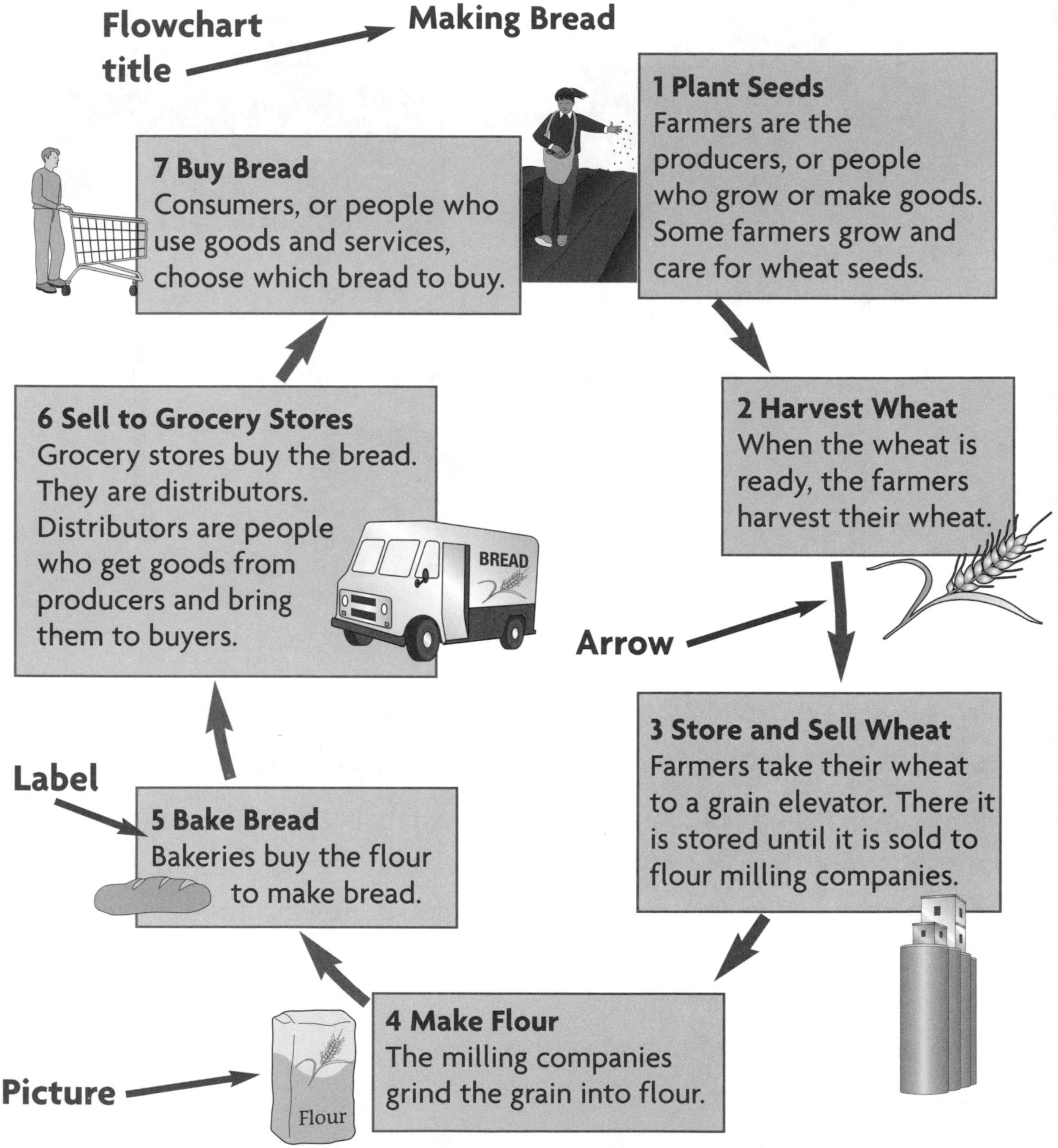

Flowchart title → Making Bread

1 Plant Seeds
Farmers are the producers, or people who grow or make goods. Some farmers grow and care for wheat seeds.

2 Harvest Wheat
When the wheat is ready, the farmers harvest their wheat.

Arrow

3 Store and Sell Wheat
Farmers take their wheat to a grain elevator. There it is stored until it is sold to flour milling companies.

4 Make Flour
The milling companies grind the grain into flour.

Picture

Label

5 Bake Bread
Bakeries buy the flour to make bread.

6 Sell to Grocery Stores
Grocery stores buy the bread. They are distributors. Distributors are people who get goods from producers and bring them to buyers.

7 Buy Bread
Consumers, or people who use goods and services, choose which bread to buy.

USE THIS SKILL

Read a Flowchart

Use the flowchart on page 194 to answer the following questions.

1. What does the title tell you about the flowchart?
2. How many steps are shown in the flowchart?
3. What is the name for people who get goods from producers and bring them to buyers?
4. Who grows or makes goods in this flowchart?
5. What steps come after baking bread?
6. Where is wheat stored until it is sold to flour milling companies?

TEST TIP

You may be asked to read a flowchart on a test. Remember that a flowchart may not be in a straight line. If there are no numbers, follow the arrows with your finger.

Skill 40

HOW TO

Make a Graphic Organizer

A Citizen's Rights and Responsibilities

In the United States, people have the freedom to do and say many things. There are many rights that the citizens of the United States have.

A **citizen** is a person who is a member of a place, such as a state or country. A citizen's rights are the things that the citizen is allowed to do. A citizen's responsibilities are the things that the citizens should do.

Citizens have rights and responsibilities.

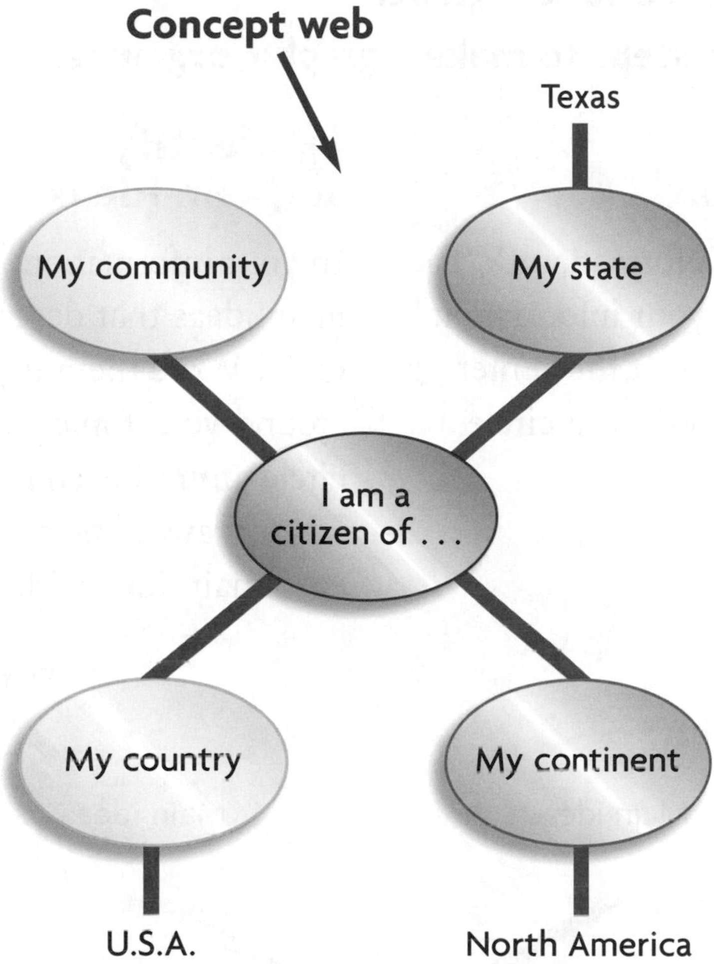

To help you learn about rights and responsibilities, you can make a graphic organizer. A **graphic organizer** is a set of lines or shapes that helps you collect and organize information.

A concept web is one kind of graphic organizer. It connects main ideas and details to a topic. A concept web, like the one above, can help you show how information is related.

STEPS IN Making a Graphic Organizer

Follow these steps to make a graphic organizer.

1 Identify Your Topic

Look at your information. What is the topic of your information? Write your topic at the center of the page and draw a circle around it.

2 Identify Main Ideas

In your information, find the main ideas that describe your topic. Write them in the space around your topic. Draw a circle around each main idea. Then draw a line to connect each main idea with the topic.

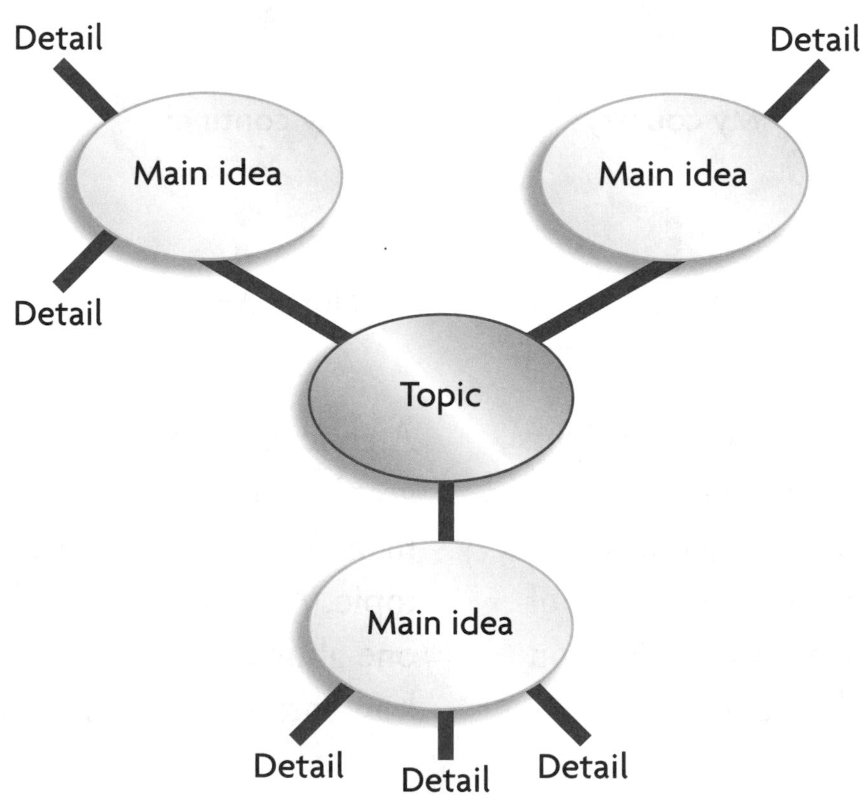

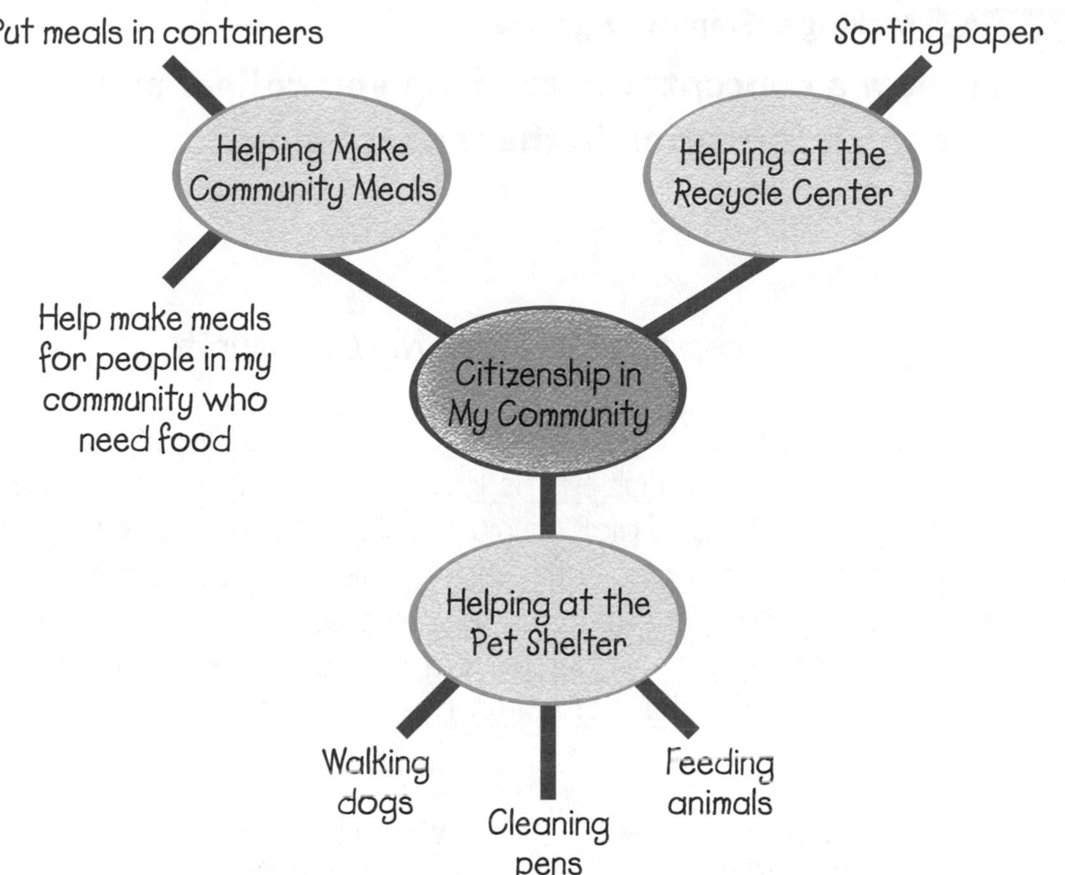

3 Connect Details

Look at your information. Decide if there are any details about the main ideas that you want to show on your concept web. Write the details next to the main ideas. Connect each detail to its main idea with a line.

TIP When making a concept web you can add color. Color can be used to show how parts of the concept web are similar or different.

EXAMPLE OF **Making a Graphic Organizer**

Look at how a concept web can help you collect and organize the information in the report below.

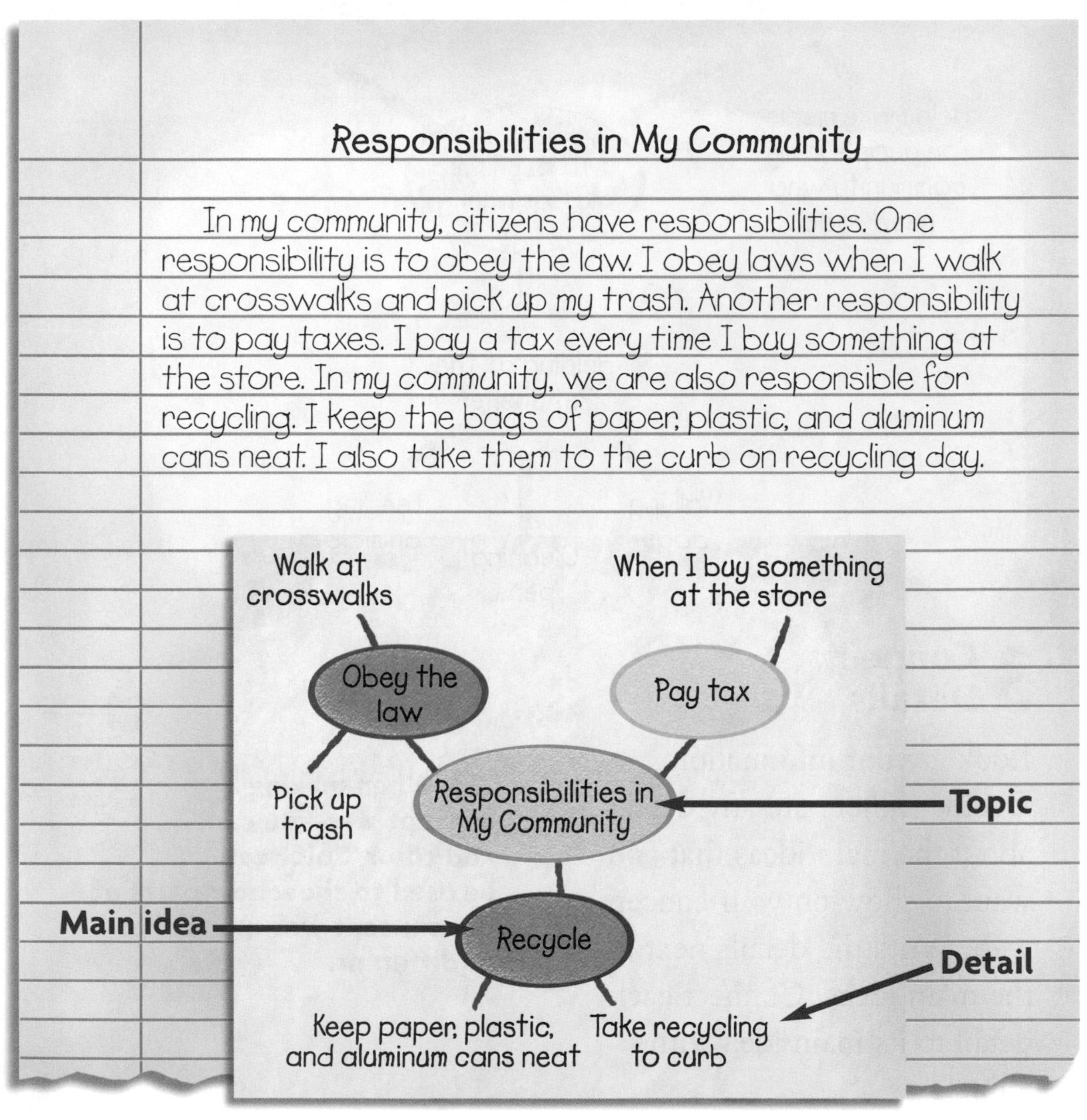

USE THIS SKILL

Make a Graphic Organizer

Use the information below to make a concept web to show how the information in the paragraph is related.

Citizen Rights

These are some rights that citizens have: free speech, voting, freedom of religion, and freedom to travel. The right to free speech means that you are free to say what you think and feel. You are free to speak your mind in public and at home. Freedom of religion is the right to practice your religion. There are many different kinds of religions practiced in the United States. Freedom to travel is the right to go from place to place.

TEST TIP

On a test, you may be asked to write an essay. Before writing, make a graphic organizer to organize your thoughts. This will help you write a good essay.

Test-Taking Strategies

Test-Taking Strategy

READING CAREFULLY

The first rule of taking a test is to read each question carefully. If you don't read the questions carefully, you will probably make a mistake.

Read the paragraph below.

You may know that the Pilgrims landed in America in 1620. Did you know that other European settlers had been in America years before? English colonists created a settlement in North Carolina in 1587. Spanish explorers founded Santa Fe in 1610.

Read each question. Find the word in each question that does not belong.

1. In which year was Santa Fe soon started?
2. Which of these cities was founded last in 1610?
3. How long before the Pilgrims landed did the English often settle in North Carolina?

How to find the answer:

- Read each question word-by-word.
- Find the word that doesn't fit with the rest of the question.
- The words that don't belong are: 1. soon, 2. last, 3. often.

It is just as important to read each answer choice carefully. You should read the answer choices word-by-word. Then think about what each answer choice means and compare it to the question.

Answer this question about the paragraph you read on the previous page.

1. Which of these is **not** mentioned in the paragraph?

   A. European settlers

   B. English colonists

   C. Spanish explorers

   D. Pilgrim soldiers

How to find the answer:

- Read every word in each answer choice.
- Compare the answer choices to the same words in the paragraph. Answers **A, B,** and **C** are in the paragraph, so they cannot be the right answer.
- Only answer **D** is **not** mentioned in the paragraph. Pilgrims are mentioned in the first sentence, but soldiers are not. That means answer **D** is correct. Only one word in answer **D** makes it wrong. Always be sure to read each word in an answer choice.

Test-Taking Strategy

IDENTIFYING DETAILS

Details are the pieces of information in a story. Detail questions usually ask about people, places, things, or times. Questions about details are usually easy to answer. You can always find the answer in the story.

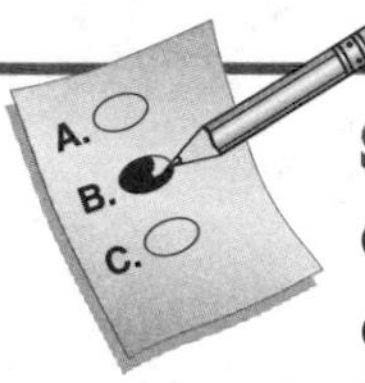

STRATEGY TIP When you read a story on a test, don't try to memorize all the facts. When you come to a detail question, go back and compare it with the story.

Read the paragraph below.

Boats made of reeds have been made in Africa for many thousands of years. Reeds are tall plants that grow in shallow water. To make a boat, the reeds are dried and tied together into bundles. Then the bundles are formed into the shape of a boat. Reed boats are very strong. Some scientists believe that long ago, people crossed the Atlantic Ocean from Africa to North America in reed boats.

Answer the question.

1. Which of these is a detail from the paragraph?

   A. Most boats are made of reeds.

   B. Boats made of reeds are not very strong.

   C. A person can't cross an ocean in a reed boat.

   D. Reeds grow in shallow water.

How to find the answer:

Compare each answer choice to the paragraph.

- The story does not say that most boats are made of reeds. Answer **A** is wrong.
- The story says that reed boats are very strong. This makes answer **B** wrong.
- The story does not say that a person cannot cross an ocean in a reed boat. Answer **C** is wrong.
- Answer **D** is correct. The second sentence says that reeds grow in shallow water.

STRATEGY TIP Sometimes an answer choice is a fact, but it is not a fact from the story. This would make it a wrong answer to a detail question.

Test-Taking Strategy

FINDING THE MAIN IDEA

The main idea is what a story is mostly about. The main idea is almost never stated in a story. You have to think about the whole story. Main idea questions ask you to tell which answer best tells what the story is about.

Read the journal entry below.

September 21, 1842

Yesterday we woke up at four o'clock. We walked through brush and logs and rocks until twelve o'clock. Then we began to climb the mountain. We only traveled one mile. When we got to the top of the mountain, it was raining and snowing. I was so wet and cold. It seems like we will never get to Oregon.

Answer the question.

1. What is this journal entry mostly about?

   A. A hike in a state park

   B. A tall mountain

   C. Walking through brush, logs, and rocks

   D. A difficult trip to Oregon

How to find the answer:

This is a main idea question, even if the words "main idea" are not in the question. Think about the paragraph and how you could explain what it is about. Look for the answer choice that tells what the story is mostly about. Don't confuse details with the main idea.

- Answer **A** can't be right. The paragraph says nothing about a state park. The right answer must be about the paragraph.
- The paragraph talks about a tall mountain, but this is just one detail. Answer **B** can't be right.
- Answer **C** can't be right for the same reason. It is just a detail in the paragraph.
- The paragraph is mostly about "A difficult trip to Oregon." This is a "big idea" that tells about the whole paragraph, not just a small part of it. Answer **D** is correct.

Test-Taking Strategy
PROCESS OF ELIMINATION

Sometimes you will know that an answer choice isn't right. When this happens, you can eliminate or cross out the answer choice. When you eliminate an answer choice, it is easier to find the right answer because you have fewer answers to choose from.

Read the paragraph below.

Did you know that geographers often use imaginary lines on a map or globe? One of these lines is called the equator. It goes around the middle of Earth like a belt between the Northern and the Southern Hemispheres. Another line is called the prime meridian. It stretches from the North Pole to the South Pole and divides the Eastern and Western Hemispheres.

Answer the question.

1. Which of these statements is true?

   A. The equator and the prime meridian are the same thing.

   B. The equator is between the Northern and Southern Hemispheres.

   C. The prime meridian goes around Earth like a belt.

   D. The equator is 100,000 miles long.

How to find the answer:

- You can quickly eliminate answer **A.** The paragraph tells how the equator and prime meridian are different.
- Answer **B** is probably correct because the paragraph says that the equator is between the Northern and Southern Hemispheres. Just to be sure, look at the rest of the answer choices.
- You can eliminate answer **C.** The paragraph says that the equator goes around the middle of Earth like a belt.
- Answer choice **D** can't be eliminated because the paragraph doesn't say how long the equator is.
- Because you could eliminate answers **A** and **C,** you have to decide between answer choices **B** and **D.** Because the paragraph says that the equator is between the Northern and Southern Hemispheres, answer **B** must be right.

STRATEGY TIP After you eliminate one or more answer choices and still aren't sure which answer is right, make a guess from the choices that might be right.

Test-Taking Strategy

USING CHARTS

A chart contains a lot of information in a little bit of space. Charts are easy to understand if you take your time but if you hurry, you can make a mistake.

Study the chart below. This chart is about four U.S. states. It shows the year people first settled in each area, the year the area was admitted as a state, and the order in which the state was admitted.

State	*Year Settled*	*Year Admitted*	*Order Admitted*
Alabama	1702	1819	22
Alaska	1784	1959	49
Arizona	1752	1912	48
Arkansas	1686	1836	25

Use the chart to answer the question.

1. Based on the chart, which of these statements is true?

   A. Alabama was settled before Arkansas.

   B. Arizona was admitted before Alaska.

   C. Alaska was settled before Arizona.

   D. Arkansas was admitted before any other state.

How to find the answer:

Compare each answer choice to the information in the chart.

- For answer **A,** look at the *Year Settled* column. Alabama was settled in 1702. Arkansas was settled in 1686. The year 1702 is **after** 1686, so answer **A** is wrong.
- For answer **B,** look in the *Year Admitted* column. Arizona was admitted in 1912, which was **before** Alaska was admitted in 1959. Answer **B** is correct.
- For answer **C,** look in the *Year Settled* column. Alaska was settled in 1784, which is **after** 1752 when Arizona was settled. Answer **C** must be wrong.
- For answer **D** to be correct, Arkansas must have the lowest number in the *Order Admitted* column. On the chart, you can see that Alabama has the lowest number so Alabama was admitted **before** Arkansas. Answer **D** must be wrong.

STRATEGY TIP Charts always contain more information than you need to answer a question. Don't let this extra information confuse you.

Test-Taking Strategy

USING GRAPHS

A graph is similar to a chart. It is a way to show a lot of information in a little bit of space. When you answer graph questions, you have to match information shown at the left of the graph with information shown at the bottom of the graph.

Study the graph below.

The graph shows how many states there were in the United States over the past 200 years in 50-year periods.

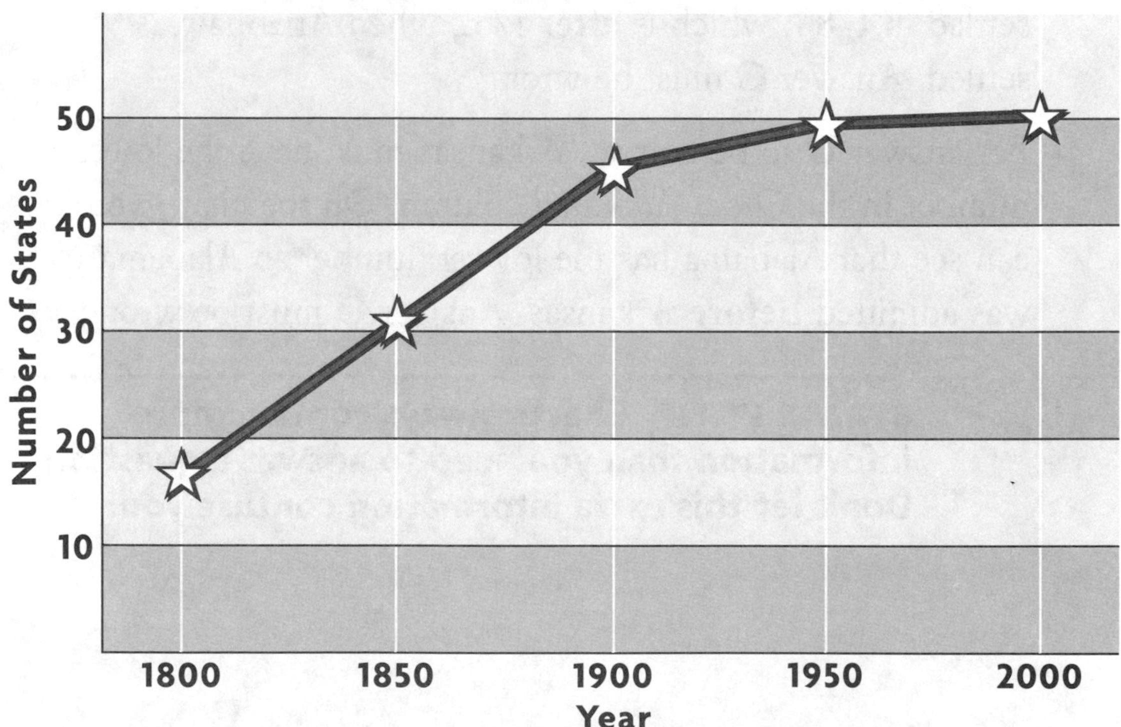

Use the graph to answer the question.

1. How many states joined the United States between 1850 and 1900?

   A. About 15

   B. About 30

   C. More than 30

   D. Less than 10

How to find the answer:

Look at the graph carefully.

- In 1850, there were about 31 states. In 1900, there were 45. This means about 14 states joined the United States between 1850 and 1900. You get this answer by subtracting 31 from 45. Answer **A** is probably right because 14 is **about** the same as 15. Just to be sure, you should check the other answers.
- Answer **B** is wrong because 30 is much more than 14.
- Answer **C** must also be wrong because more than 30 is much more than 14.
- Answer **D** is "Less than 10." The number 14 is more than 10. Therefore, answer **D** is wrong.

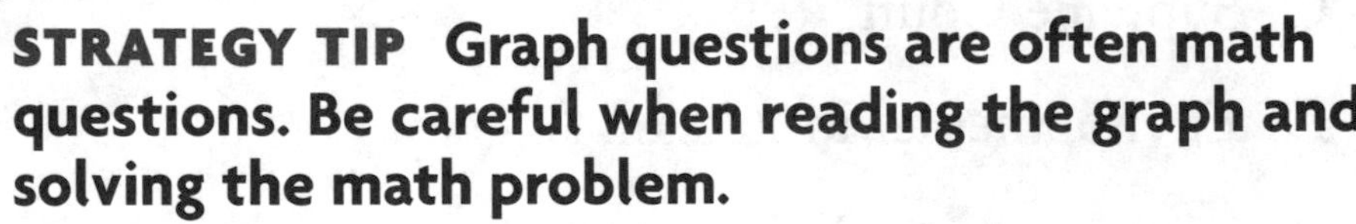

Test-Taking Strategy

STAYING WITH THE FIRST ANSWER

On a test, the first answer you choose is usually correct. Even if you aren't sure which answer is correct, your first answer is right more often than it is wrong.

Read the paragraph below and answer the question.

The United States has three branches of government. The legislative branch makes the laws. It includes the Senate and House of Representatives. The executive branch carries out the laws. The president is the head of the executive branch of the government. The judicial branch includes the Supreme Court. It explains laws and makes sure that laws make sense. This system of three branches was created for an important reason. It makes sure that no person or group has too much power.

1. The United States has many laws to protect the environment. Which branch of government decides if these laws are fair?

   A. Senate and House of Representatives

   B. President

   C. Supreme Court

   D. Environmental Protection Agency

How to find the answer:

The key words **decides if these laws are fair** are not in the paragraph. So, look for words that mean the same thing.

- The Senate and House of Representatives **make laws,** not decide if they are fair. Answer **A** is probably wrong.
- The president **carries out laws.** This is **not** the same as deciding if they are fair, so answer **B** is probably wrong.
- The Supreme Court makes **sure that laws make sense.** This means about the same thing as decides if laws are fair. So far, answer **C** is the best answer.
- Answer **D,** Environmental Protection Agency, isn't in the paragraph so this answer is wrong.
- The best answer is **C.** If you weren't sure **C** was right, you might have picked answer **D** because of the word **environmental.** This is why you should stay with your first answer unless you are sure another one is better.

Test-Taking Strategy

ORDER AND SEQUENCE

Sometimes a graphic will show the order in which things happen. The information on a time line or flowchart is arranged according to time. Like a story, it can have a beginning, middle, and end. It is important that you pay attention to this order when you try to answer questions.

Study the time line below.

The time line shows the dates of different explorations.

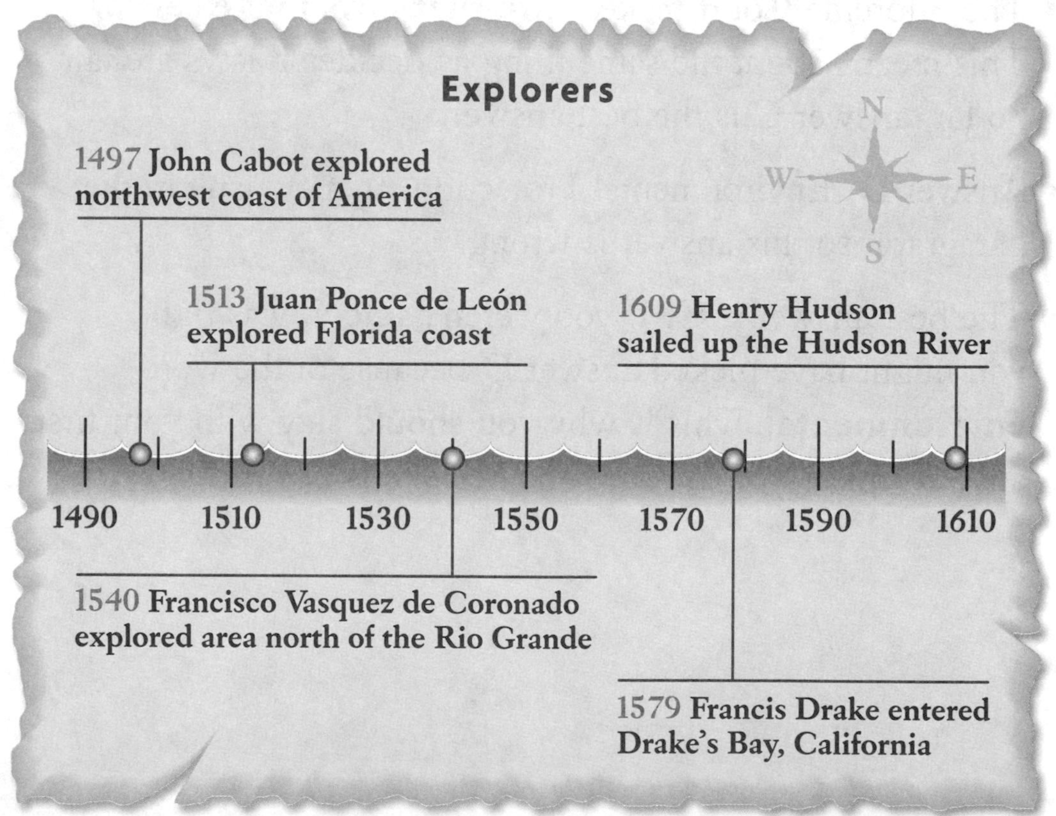

Use the time line to answer the question.

1. Hernando de Soto landed in Florida in 1539. Which person made an exploration just after de Soto?

   A. John Cabot

   B. Francis Drake

   C. Juan Ponce de León

   D. Francisco Vasquez de Coronado

How to find the answer:

Look at the time line and find the explorer whose date is closest to dc Soto but **after** his exploration in 1539.

- Cabot's exploration was **before** 1539, so **A** is wrong.
- Drake's exploration was **after** 1539. Answer **B** might be the right answer, but another answer might be better. Let's keep looking.
- Answer **C** can't be right because Ponce de León's exploration was in 1513, which was **before** 1539.
- The exploration of Coronado took place in 1540. This is **after** de Soto. The Coronado date is also much closer to the de Soto date than Drake's exploration. This means answer **D** is correct.

GLOSSARY

A

advertisement something that tells about a product or service

assembly line a way of making something by having the item being made move along a path to workers who build certain parts

B

bar graph a kind of drawing that uses rectangles called bars to show information

biography a story about a person's life

boundary a line where one thing ends and something else begins

business letter a letter with a serious purpose

business plan a plan that tells what people starting a business are going to do and how they will do it

C

cardinal directions the directions North, South, East, and West

cause the reason why something happens

chart a set of lines or a drawing that organizes information

citizen a person who is a member of a place, such as a state or country

classify put things into groups

community a place where people live, work, and play

community map a map that shows the features of a community

compare tell how people, places, or things are alike

comparison a writing that tells how two or more things are alike

compass rose shows directions on a map

conclusion a statement that sums up the meaning of information in a picture or story

contrast tell how people, places, or things are different

country map a map that shows information about a country

cultural map a map that shows where people sharing the same culture live or lived

culture a group of people's way of life

D

decision a choice you make

diagram a drawing that shows the parts of something

E

effect what happens after a cause

encyclopedia a set of books with articles on many topics

equator the line around the middle of Earth, halfway between the North and South Poles

explanation telling how something is done

F

fact a statement that is true

factory a building or set of buildings in which things are made

flowchart a kind of drawing that shows the steps in a process

G

globe a model of Earth

goods things people make

graphic organizer a set of lines or shapes that helps you collect and organize information

grid map a map with lines that divide the map into smaller parts

H

historical map a map that gives information about the past

I

intermediate directions the directions in between cardinal directions: Northwest, Northeast, Southwest, and Southeast

Internet a network that lets computers share information

interview a meeting in which one person asks questions and another person answers them

J

job the work that a person does

journal a kind of notebook in which you write your thoughts, feelings, and memories

K

L

legend shows what the different features on a map stand for

line graph a kind of drawing that uses a line to show how something changes over time

M

manufacture make something by putting materials together by hand or with a machine

map a flat drawing that shows what a real place looks like from above

map key shows what different features on a map stand for

map scale line that helps to measure distance on a map

map title tells you what the map shows

N

O

opinion a statement telling what a person, thinks, believes, or feels

oral report a spoken report that shares information about a subject

outline a list that organizes information by showing a topic, main ideas, and details

P

paragraph a group of two or more sentences about one subject

patriotic holiday a holiday that honors a part of your country's history

plantations large farms on which many people in the southern United States lived in the 1700s

point of view the way a person looks at something based on his or her ideas, feelings, and experiences

prime meridian the line that goes around Earth from the North Pole to the South Pole

Q

R

recycle help turn waste material back into useful products

reduce use less of something

reference sources books or other sources that give useful information about a topic

reuse find new uses for something

road map a map that shows the roads in an area

S

services things people do

skit a short play

state map a map that shows information about a state

summary a writing that tells the main ideas of something

symbols small drawings that are used on a map, such as pictures, colors, and shapes

T

take notes write down important information about a topic to help you remember it later

time line a line that shows the order in which events happened

U

V

W

Web site all of the words and images that a group shows on the Internet

working in a group two or more people helping each other achieve a goal

X

Y

Z

INDEX

D

E

F

G

H

T

U

V

W

Y

Z

Credits

Cover ©Leif Skoogfors/Corbis; **28** ©Photo Library International/Science Photo Library/ Photo Researchers, Inc.; **29** PhotoDisc; **47 (t)** ©Lawrence Migdale **(b)** ©Richard A. Cooke/Corbis; **50** ©Thomas S. England/Photo Researchers, Inc.; **63 (l)** ©Tom Bean/ Corbis, **(r)** ©Macduff Everton/Corbis; **65, 69** ©Bettmann/Corbis; **70** Denver Public Library, Colorado Historical Society and Denver Art Museum; **74, 77, 79** ©Corbis; **80** PhotoDisc; **81** ©Michael Newman/PhotoEdit; **87** ©AFP/Corbis; **92** ©Bettmann/ Corbis; **104, 106** ©Corbis; **108** ©1995 N. Carter/North Wind Picture Archive; **111** PhotoDisc; **112** ©The Granger Collection; **115 (l)** ©The Granger Collection, **(r)** Paul Conklin/PhotoEdit; **116** ©Bettmann/Corbis; **121** ©Deborah Davis/PhotoEdit; **130** ©Bettmann/Corbis; **140** ©Mark Richards/PhotoEdit; **141, 144** Courtesy of The White House; **150** ©Bettmann/Corbis; **152** Museum of the City of New York, Scala/Art Resource, NY; **156** ©Bettmann/Corbis; **157** ©The Granger Collection; **158** ©Francis G. Mayer/ Corbis; **162** ©Kim Heacox/Tony Stone; **163** ©The Granger Collection; **172 (l)** ©Kim Sayer/Corbis, **(c)** Courtesy of Lego, Inc., **(r)** PhotoDisc; **173 (l)** Photograph ©Jeff Potacsnak, **(r)** ©2001 Mattel, Inc; **184** ©Rykoff Collection/Corbis; **187** ©Bettmann/Corbis; **196** ©Steve Chenn/Corbis.